JUMP START RAILS

BY ANDY HAWTHORNE

Jump Start Rails

by Andy Hawthorne

Product Manager: Simon Mackie
English Editor: Paul Fitzpatrick
Technical Editor: Glenn Goodrich
Cover Designer: Alex Walker

Notice of Rights

Notice of Liability

Trademark Notice

Published by SitePoint Pty. Ltd.

48 Cambridge Street Collingwood
VIC Australia 3066
Web: www.sitepoint.com
Email: business@sitepoint.com

ISBN 978-0-9874674-2-3 (print)

ISBN 978-0-9874674-3-0 (ebook)
Printed and bound in the United States of America

About Andy Hawthorne

Andy is a freelance writer and web developer from Coventry, England. He has spent 12 years as a web developer, and still likes trying new web coding technologies.

About SitePoint

SitePoint specializes in publishing fun, practical, and easy-to-understand content for web professionals. Visit http://www.sitepoint.com/ to access our blogs, books, newsletters, articles, and community forums. You'll find a stack of information on JavaScript, PHP, Ruby, mobile development, design, and more.

About Jump Start

Jump Start books provide you with a rapid and practical introduction to web development languages and technologies. Typically around 150 pages in length, they can be read in a weekend, giving you a solid grounding in the topic and the confidence to experiment on your own.

To my wife Mary— without her never-failing love and support I'd never get anything finished. And to my Dad, who inspired me to write in the first place.

Table of Contents

Preface

Ruby on Rails was created in 2003 by David Heinemeier Hansson. Since then it has been extended by more than 21,000 contributors.

Rails was always intended to make web development a much slicker process than was previously available with other technologies. It doesn't require thousands of lines of code to get common functionality built into your apps. Rails uses the concept of "convention over configuration", meaning that many of the common tasks we do when developing web applications are covered quickly and easily.

It is true to say that Rails has a steeper learner curve than, say, your average PHP framework. However, the effort to learn it is certainly worth it. I doubt that you will ever fully go back to choosing other technologies over Rails where it makes sense for the app you are building.

The Ruby programming language is a delight to work with, too. It's what Rails is built on, and it offers a powerful set of features for all sorts of programming tasks, not just those for the Web.

This is a short book, designed to give you a "jump start" with Rails. I've based it on my own experiences of building a production Rails app for the first time. Hopefully, like me, you will come to enjoy the slick, efficient web development experience that Rails provides.

Who Should Read This Book

Developers seeking a rapid introduction to Rails. You'll need to know HTML and CSS, and experience with other programming languages would be useful.

Conventions Used

You'll notice that we've used certain typographic and layout styles throughout this book to signify different types of information. Look out for the following items.

Code Samples

Code in this book will be displayed using a fixed-width font, like so:

```
<h1>A Perfect Summer's Day</h1>
<p>It was a lovely day for a walk in the park. The birds
were singing and the kids were all back at school.</p>
```

If the code is to be found in the book's code archive, the name of the file will appear at the top of the program listing, like this:

example.css

```
.footer {
  background-color: #CCC;
  border-top: 1px solid #333;
}
```

If only part of the file is displayed, this is indicated by the word *excerpt*:

example.css *(excerpt)*

```
  border-top: 1px solid #333;
```

If additional code is to be inserted into an existing example, the new code will be displayed in bold:

```
function animate() {
  new_variable = "Hello";
}
```

Also, where existing code is required for context, rather than repeat all the code, a ⋮ will be displayed:

```
function animate() {
  ⋮
  return new_variable;
}
```

Some lines of code are intended to be entered on one line, but we've had to wrap them because of page constraints. A ➥ indicates a line break that exists for formatting purposes only, and should be ignored.

```
URL.open("http://www.sitepoint.com/responsive-web-design-real-user-
➥testing/?responsive1");
```

Tips, Notes, and Warnings

Hey, You!

Tips will give you helpful little pointers.

Ahem, Excuse Me ...

Notes are useful asides that are related—but not critical—to the topic at hand. Think of them as extra tidbits of information.

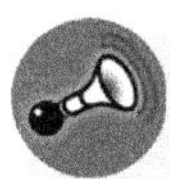

Make Sure You Always ...

... pay attention to these important points.

Watch Out!

Warnings will highlight any gotchas that are likely to trip you up along the way.

Supplementary Materials

http://www.sitepoint.com/books/jsrails1/
The book's website, containing links, updates, resources, and more.

http://www.sitepoint.com/books/jsrails1/code.php
The downloadable code archive for this book.

http://www.sitepoint.com/forums/forumdisplay.php?227-Ruby-amp-Rails
SitePoint's forums, for help on any tricky web problems.

`books@sitepoint.com`
Our email address, should you need to contact us for support, to report a problem, or for any other reason.

Do you want to keep learning?

You can now get unlimited access to courses and ALL SitePoint books at Learnable for one low price. Enroll now and start learning today! Join Learnable and you'll stay ahead of the newest technology trends: http://www.learnable.com.

Once you've mastered the principles of Rails, challenge yourself with our online quiz. Can you achieve a perfect score? Head on over to http://quizpoint.com/#categories/RUBY.

Chapter 1

Getting on Rails

Welcome to Jump Start Rails! If you've come to Rails from another server-side coding technology such as PHP, you are in for a treat. Rails offers a slick and efficient coding experience for web developers, and was created with built-in solutions to many of the common web development headaches.

Rails is open source and free to use, which means that you don't need to spend a lot to get developing with it. In fact, the biggest outlay will probably be purchasing an editor. We'll look at the options a little later in this chapter.

Rails was created in 2003 by David Heinemeier Hansson of 37 Signals[1] fame. Since then, it has seen rapid development by the Rails core team[2], with over 2,000 contributors. Rails runs on the Ruby[3] general purpose programming language, created by Yukihiro "Matz" Matsumoto, in 1995.

[1] http://37signals.com/

[2] http://rubyonrails.org/core

[3] http://www.ruby-lang.org/en/

Do I need to know Ruby?

You can certainly build simple Rails apps with a *limited* knowledge of Ruby. Many developers tend to learn Ruby as they learn Rails. And as your knowledge and confidence with Rails increases, you'll want to do more with it.

I've found that you can do this in incremental steps; it's entirely possible to build a Rails app while you are still learning Ruby. The good news is that learning Rails is a great experience, but learning Ruby is equally rewarding — especially if you have come from another language like PHP, for example. Ruby is described on the Ruby website[4] as "a programmer's best friend" for a reason. So to really get into Rails a good knowledge of Ruby will be required — eventually.

Ruby seems to be built for learning on the go—whenever you come across an obstacle, the answer is never far away. Ruby Docs[5] will help enormously with this.

What You'll Need

Ruby on Rails[6], like many other web coding technologies, requires some setting up on your system first. It's not too scary, though, and since this book covers Rails 4.0, we only have to be concerned with setting up to use the latest versions.

Rails isn't Ruby. It's built *using* Ruby, and you use Ruby to build Rails applications. As such, it needs to be present on your system for Rails to run. Happily Ruby is available to run pretty much everywhere.

The Rails Stack

There are several components that make up the Rails stack. Obviously Ruby is one component, the other main one being a database of some kind.

During the process of guiding you through installing Rails in this chapter, I'll mention PostgreSQL[7] and Ruby Version Manager (RVM)[8]. Technically neither are *essential* requirements; it's just that they are common tools used in creating a Rails stack.

---

[4] http://www.ruby-lang.org/en/

[5] http://ruby-doc.org/core-1.9.3/

[6] http://rubyonrails.org/

[7] http://www.postgresql.org/

[8] http://rvm.io

RVM is a sandboxed way to install numerous versions of Ruby on your system, all without affecting any system configuration files. It's available for Unix-based systems, and as part of an installer[9] for Windows.

If you create a Rails project without specifying a database, one will be created anyway. It'll be a SQLite database[10], and will serve very well for your initial Rails investigation. However, in Chapter 6, we'll be deploying to Heroku[11], and that requires a PostgreSQL database[12]. As such, we'll be making PostgreSQL part of our Rails stack too.

Rails and MVC

The Rails framework is based on the Model View Controller (MVC) design pattern. No doubt you'll have heard of it if you've already spent time around web development. The truth is that, with Rails, there are real advantages to be had from MVC.

A few of these advantages are:

- the ability to keep application logic (or business logic, if you prefer) separate from the user interface
- Don't Repeat Yourself (DRY) capability. The term DRY also applies in all forms of web and software development. It's a concept where the objective is to only write one piece of code to perform a particular task. You'll see this in action as we begin to build our main app
- a clear pattern for where each type of code should be stored within the application

Rails uses MVC like this:

- **Models** are used mostly for setting the rules for interaction with database tables. Normally, you would have one model per database table.

---

[9] http://railsinstaller.org/
[10] http://www.sqlite.org/
[11] http://www.heroku.com/
[12] http://www.postgresql.org/

- **Views** are HTML files with Ruby embedded to perform tasks for the presentation of data. Views are the user interface the part of your app with which the user interacts.

- **Controllers** are the components that decide how to respond to user requests. They are responsible for coordinating responses too. You can think of them as traffic police directing requests and responses around the application. It's important to understand that controllers are the only components that can speak to models and views, as well as to our user's browser.

Installing Rails

Let's run through the basic process of getting Rails installed on Windows, Mac, and Linux.

Installing Rails on Windows

I'm going to stick my neck out here: If you intend to work seriously with Rails, then you might want to consider switching to a Unix-based operating system. The reason is a practical one: You'll be spending a lot time on the command line with Rails. You will also need to keep your Ruby gems up to date. This is all done via the command line. The fact is, it's far easier to manage this stuff on a Unix system such as Linux or Mac OS X. You could always run a Virtual Machine for your Rails-coding projects, and I'll explain how to do that later in this chapter.

There are options for Windows users, and it's worth mentioning that huge efforts are being made to make Ruby easier to work with on Windows.

If you are running Windows, there is now an easy solution for getting going with Rails. The RailsInstaller[13] has been provided by the team at Engine Yard, and it takes the pain out of configuring Ruby and Rails manually. Simply download the installer, run it, and away you go.

The installer includes all of the required gems and dependencies so that you can start using Rails immediately. It even includes Git, the version control system, widely used in the Ruby/Rails community.

---

[13] http://railsinstaller.org/

PostgreSQL Database

You can download the required software from the PostgreSQL[14]. It includes the excellent pgAdmin tool—a graphical user interface for the database. You just need to download and install the software and leave it at that. There is very little else to do, as you will work with the database mostly via Rails.

When we get to deployment, I'll explain how you can import and export data between your local PostgreSQL installation and the server running at Heroku.

Another Option for Windows Users

There is another way of setting up for Rails development on Windows—a virtual machine (VM). It's a more involved process, but if you want to try Linux, this is one way to do it.

For example, there is an excellent open source package available for Windows, called VirtualBox[15]. VirtualBox provides you with the required base in which you're free to create as many virtual machines as your system can handle. The idea is that you install whichever flavor of Linux takes your fancy, install Ruby/Rails and the associated requirements, and do your development in the VM, rather than on your base system.

The advantage of this approach is that you don't have to install any of the required components on your base system so, should anything go awry, you can simply delete the VM and start again. Your base system is not affected in any way.

So, how do we do it? First, you'll have some downloading to do, and it certainly helps if you have installed a Linux distribution (distro for short) before. Here are the steps:

1. Download the ISO for your chosen Linux distro. I always store mine in a folder called **iso** in my **Home** directory—it makes it easier to find when you create your VM.

2. Download VirtualBox, and install it. This should prove to be just a normal installation, like any other software.

---

[14] http://www.postgresql.org/download/windows/

[15] https://www.virtualbox.org/wiki/Downloads

3. Create a new VM, and select the ISO file you downloaded as the source. The ISO file for various flavors of Linux can be found at their respective sites. For Ubuntu, for example, head to Ubuntu's download page[16] and follow the instructions to download Ubuntu Desktop.

4. Once you have the ISO file, you can create a new VM and mount the ISO file, which will boot into the installation program. Installing Ubuntu, for example, is not difficult, but you may hit a speed bump or two. If you do, search the Web for "installing Ubuntu on VirtualBox" for an avalanche of information.

There is an article on RubySource that demonstrates how to create a functional Rails development environment using VirtualBox here[17].

It's worth mentioning that you can install VirtualBox on most platforms, including Linux. Once you have completed the above steps, you can jump in and install Rails for Linux, which is covered in the next section.

Installing on GNU Linux

Most Linux distros come with Ruby installed, but there's a good chance that this will be Ruby 1.8.7. While this is okay for older versions of Rails, we are using the latest, Rails 4.0, so we need Ruby 1.9.3 or higher. And for the purposes of this book we'll be using 2.0.

At the time of writing, there isn't a Rails Installer version for Linux, although there is one planned. So for now, we'll have to do it ourselves. It's not difficult, though, and as long as you're careful about installing the dependencies, you'll have a trouble-free Rails installation running via RVM in no time.

The steps to install RVM vary from distro to distro. I'm going to cover installation on the popular Ubuntu distro (version 12.10).

This routine will work on a fresh Ubuntu installation (so if you are installing in a VM it'll work just fine), and I've also followed the same steps on older installations of Ubuntu 12.10.

---

[16] http://ubuntu.com/download

[17] ???

Right, down to business. I've gone through this process with a clean Ubuntu installation running in a VM. We'll be doing everything via the Terminal, so fire it up, and install curl:

```
sudo apt-get install curl
```

Likewise, we'll be needing Git for version control because that's how we deploy to Heroku, and we need some essential tools to help us build some of the gems:

```
sudo apt-get install git-core build-essential
```

Next, we can go ahead and install RVM:

```
curl -L get.rvm.io | bash -s stable
```

When the installation completes, RVM provides you with essential information about requirements and dependencies that need to be satisfied to run Ruby properly. You can see what you need with:

```
rvm requirements
```

You'll get a list of dependencies that **must** be installed. The list will look something like this:

```
    Additional Dependencies:
    # For Ruby / Ruby HEAD (MRI, Rubinius, & REE),
    install the  following:
    ruby: /usr/bin/apt-get install build-essential openssl
➥libreadline6 libreadline6-dev curl git-core zlib1g
➥zlib1g-dev libssl-dev libyaml-dev libsqlite3-dev sqlite3
➥libxml2-dev libxslt-dev autoconf libc6-dev ncurses-dev
➥automake libtool bison subversion pkg-config
```

You can get all these dependencies installed in one hit in Terminal, by using `apt-get`. So you would enter:

```
sudo apt-get install build-essential openssl libreadline6
➥libreadline6-dev curl git-core zlib1g zlib1g-dev libssl-dev
➥ libyaml-dev libsqlite3-dev sqlite3 libxml2-dev libxslt-dev
➥autoconf libc6-dev ncurses-dev automake libtool bison
➥subversion pkg-config
```

Please note that the list of dependencies you see may not be the same as what's shown here. Also, RVM does allow you to enable a setting that will automatically handle the requirements (`rvm autolibs enable`) if you wish. For our purposes we'll install them using `apt-get`.

Just to clear up any confusion here, you'll need to use `sudo` here, because the dependencies that are being installed are system wide. However, when we use RVM to install gems a little later, you *shouldn't* use `sudo`. That's because RVM installs on your local user account. That's why it's sandboxed and doesn't affect your system Ruby.

Next, you need to make sure that RVM is being loaded as a function. The usual method is to get on Terminal and enter:

```
source ~/.rvm/scripts/rvm
```

Re-start Terminal, and then enter:

```
type rvm | head -n 1
```

You should get: `RVM is a function` as a reply. If you do, great. If not, you'll need to follow the instructions on the RVM web site[18].

Installing Ruby

Now we can install Ruby. Enter:

```
rvm install 2.0.0
```

RVM will download and install Ruby version 2.0.0. Next, ensure your system is using the newly installed version of Ruby as the default:

---

[18] https://rvm.io/integration/gnome-terminal/

```
rvm use 2.0.0 --default
```

We should be good to install Rails now:

```
gem install rails
```

That's it! Rails is now up and running.

We can also install PostgreSQL.This can be done via apt-get in Terminal, and you'll also find it in the Ubuntu Software Centre. However, since you'll be needing the development header files and their dependencies so that you can install the `pg` gem, the easiest way to do it is to install everything you need via the Synaptic Package Manager.

That can be installed via the Ubuntu Software Centre, as shown in Figure 1.1.

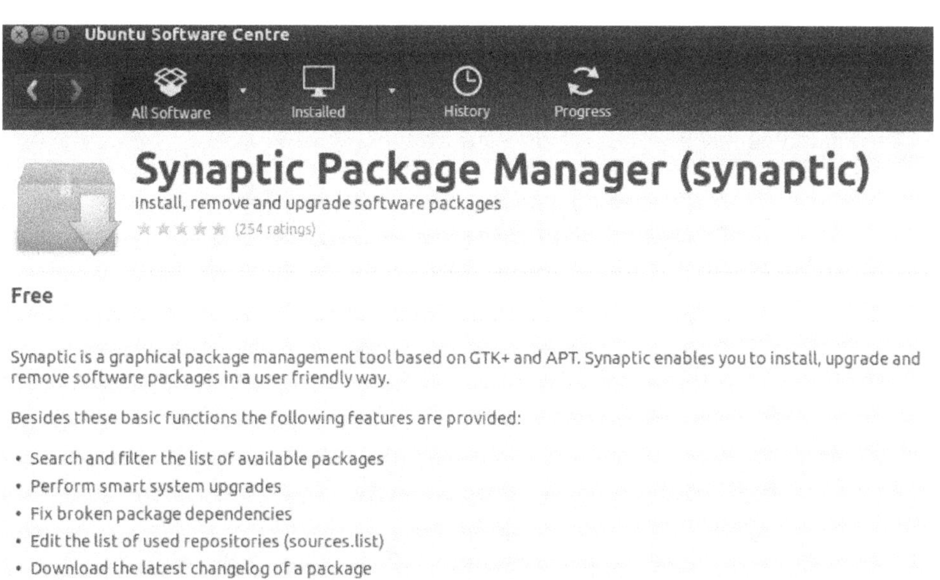

Figure 1.1. Ubuntu Software Centre

Then, via Synaptic, you can install all the components you need just by searching for them: PostgreSQL itself, a file called `postgresql-server-dev-9.1`, and pgAdmin, the GUI tool for working with PostgreSQL.

Installing Rails on Mac OS X

Macs come with Ruby installed already. The only problem is, Rails needs at least Ruby version 1.9 or higher to run and your Mac (yes, even one running Mountain Lion) comes with Ruby 1.8.7. That's the bad news.

The good news is, Engine Yard have made a version of RailsInstaller[19] for Macs too. Even better, it installs in a sandbox so it has no effect on your system Ruby. All you need to do is download the .DMG file and install it as you would any other Mac software.

RailsInstaller provides you with everything you need to start building Rails apps. Just keep in mind that the Installer adds RVM to your system so that you can easily run different versions of Ruby, and different isolated sets of gems (called, unsurprisingly, "gemsets"). As a beginner, you may not see any advantage in that, but trust me, if you've tried installation in other ways, the resulting pain is not nice at all.

You also get another treat with RailsInstaller. It comes in the shape of the JewelryBox, which is shown in Figure 1.2. It's a graphical user interface for managing the Rubies and associated gem sets you have on your system.

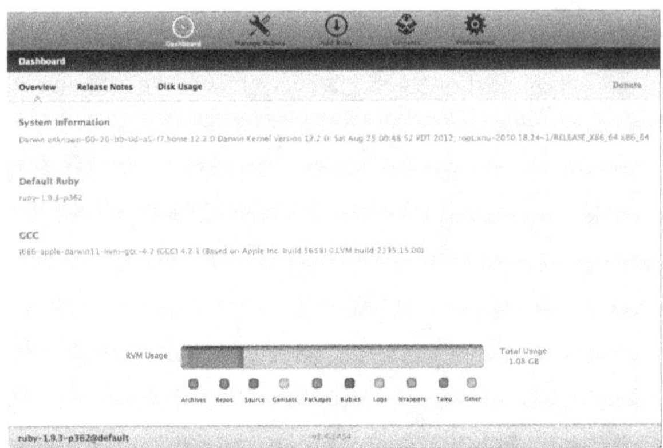

Figure 1.2. RailsInstaller JewelryBox

There are two kinds of experiences when installing gems via this set-up: hellish or easy! To avoid the hellish option, you'll be needing some compilers.

[19] http://railsinstaller.org

For OS X Mountain Lion you need software from Apple called XCode[20]. It's available on the Mac App Store[21], is free (although the download will suck up several gigabytes of data), and installs just like any other software. You'll also need the command line tools. You can use these if you are a member of the Apple developer community as a separate download. Or, you can install them directly from within XCode. You'll find the option to do so from the preferences panel (**Preferences** > **Downloads** > **Components** > **Install**), as shown in Figure 1.3.

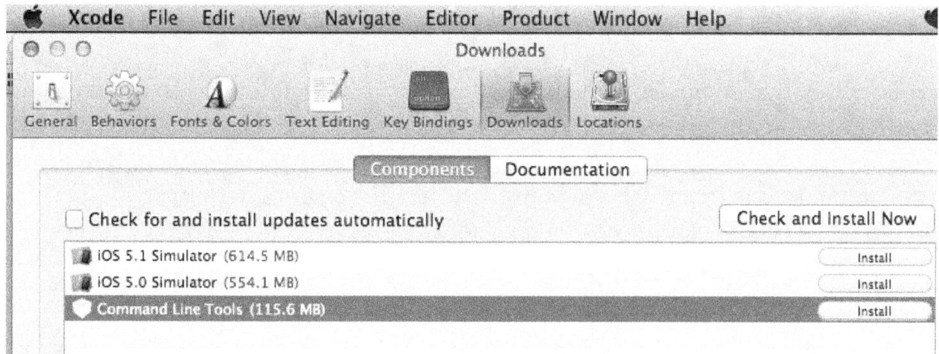

Figure 1.3. XCode command line tools

You can install just RVM without the RailsInstaller. RVM and its gemsets help you jump between Ruby versions for your Ruby applications. XCode gives you the tools that you need to compile those gems that require compilation when installed. If it seems a bit convoluted right now, rest assured, it will get clearer as you play with Ruby and Rails more.

Homebrew

If RVM helps you manage your Ruby-based dependencies (meaning, gems), Homebrew helps you manage those dependencies *outside* of Ruby. One such dependency is PostgresSQL, which I mentioned earlier.

Homebrew refers to itself as "the missing package manager for OS X", and it's a good description.

We are planning to build an app and deploy it to Heroku. For that, you'd be well advised to get used to working with PostgreSQL. And to install that, we really need

[20] https://developer.apple.com/xcode/

[21] https://itunes.apple.com/us/app/xcode/id497799835

Homebrew. There are Mac binaries available for PostgreSQL, but I don't recommend you use those for one simple reason: For the `pg` gem to install correctly, you'll need the development header files installed; you don't get them with the binary versions, but you *do* when you install via Homebrew.

To install Homebrew you should follow the instructions[22]. In a nutshell, though, you use Ruby to install it:

```
ruby -e "$(curl -fsSkL raw.github.com/mxcl/homebrew/go)"
```

Homebrew will sort out any dependency issues, and install everything in a sand-boxed environment in `/usr/local`.

Once Homebrew is installed, you can then install PostgreSQL with:

```
brew install postgresql
```

I don't recommend installing the download version of PostgreSQL from its website because you'll be missing the development files needed to install the `pg` gem. You can, however, download and install pgAdmin[23], which will help you see and manipulate the content of your databases.

Some Other Options

There are some alternatives to the options I've mentioned so far.

rbenv

For completeness, I should mention one other option for managing Rubies. It's called rbenv[24] and you can read about how it differs from RVM at its website[25].

Personally, I've always chosen RVM, and the reason is simple: allowing for the caveats mentioned in this chapter RVM gets very close to the software Nirvana of "it just works." That's not to say rbenv *doesn't* work, but since you're going to be busy mastering Rails, why add learning a different Ruby manager to your to-do list?

[22] http://mxcl.github.com/homebrew/
[23] http://www.pgadmin.org/
[24] https://github.com/sstephenson/rbenv
[25] https://github.com/sstephenson/rbenv/wiki/Why-rbenv%3F

Databases

If you don't specify a different database, Rails will use SQLite by default. Since will deploy to Heroku, I'm going to use PostgreSQL for the main app we build in this book.

It's worth mentioning that you do have the option to develop using SQLite and still deploy to Heroku. However, keep in mind that you cannot use SQLite on Heroku. So the best way to dovolop locally using SQLite, and deploy to Heroku's PostgreSQL server, is to make a change in your Gemfile. We'll cover how to do that in the next section.

Installing Ruby Gems

Now that you are running RVM, it's worth pointing out that adding other gems is easy. For example, if you type the following at the command line the Thin gem will be installed:

```
gem install thin
```

"Thin," by the way, is another web server for running Rails applications.

Rails, along with most Ruby gems and applications, doesn'tt require you to manually install each gem at the command line. To do this you can use Bundler[26]. If you place all the gems you need into a file called "Gemfile" in the root of your application, Bundler will install them all with a simple command. You'll see this in action soon.

If you were going to use SQLite for local development, then before you deployed to Heroku, you would need to make a change in your Gemfile like this:

```
group :production, :staging do
  gem "pg"
end
```

[26] http://gembundler.com/

```
group :development, :test do
  gem "sqlite3-ruby", "~> 1.3.0", :require => "sqlite3"
end
```

This ensures that you are using the pg (short for PostgreSQL) gem when running on Heroku, and SQLite when working locally, and demonstrates how important the Gemfile is. Rails uses `Bundler` to manage a consistent environment for Ruby applications. Bundler is amazing because it tracks the gems your application needs to run, along with the versions.

Your application's Gemfile lists all the gems being used, and what version. To install all the gems in your app's Gemfile, you'd jump into Terminal and enter:

```
bundle install
```

The Gemfile has to have at least one source, but once that's in place, `bundle install` will download and install all the gems that the app needs to run. You'll see this in action throughout the book.

A Word about Editors

Choosing an editor for Rails, or for any other web development for that matter, is subjective. However, I'll offer this piece of advice: don't use an IDE, because you won't learn that way. You should also consider investing in an editor such as Sublime Text 2[27]. It's available on all platforms, which means you can work on your Windows machine, Mac, or Linux and have the same coding experience.

If you are looking for a free option, you have a couple of choices that are popular in the Ruby/Rails community. First, there is GNU Emacs[28], which has a minor mode[29] (think plugin) that's dedicated to Rails development. The other well-known free option is Vim[30]. There are versions of it available for most platforms, and there is also a dedicated Rails plugin[31]. You'll also find there are many packages specific to Rails development being added. That said, the learning curve for Emacs and Vim

---

[27] http://www.sublimetext.com/
[28] http://www.gnu.org/software/emacs/
[29] https://github.com/remvee/emacs-rails
[30] http://www.vim.org/download.php
[31] https://github.com/tpope/vim-rails

can be daunting, and most new Rails developers are already absorbing a lot of new information.

Summary

You now have Rails up and running on your computer. Most problems that arise when installing Rails have been answered, and the Rails community is friendly and helpful. In the worse-case scenario, installing via RVM means that it is easy to dump the local RVM folder and start again. However, that shouldn't be necessary as long as you've paid attention to the dependencies needed for your chosen platform.

It's time for code. So let's begin creating Rails apps to see what all the fuss is about...

Chapter 2

Starting an App

The plan, by the end of the book, is for you to have built a fully functioning Rails application—and, in this chapter, we are going to start that process. We'll do it by building a smaller *training* app—something you can refer back to and experiment with as your knowledge of Rails grows. That way, you'll get a feel for how a Rails app hangs together. You'll also become familiar with the various files and directories that make up a standard Rails app.

Data First?

It's common when building an app for the data requirements to come first. In fact, we'll be doing exactly that when we start our main project for the book—planning the database schema and creating models *are* the first tasks.

Now this might feel a bit strange if you've come from a different web language/technology, such as PHP. After all, seeing something up and running first is nice, isn't it? I remember feeling a bit flummoxed when I first started out with Rails, what with all the talk of models and schemas before I knew what the app was even going to look like. For that reason we're going to approach the training app from the front end first.

Hello, World

It's common practice when trying out a new programming technology to build something that says: "Hello, world!" Our training app will initially include a simple layout and seeing a view in action. We'll link some pages together too, so you can develop a feel for how static pages in Rails work. And while it won't *do* anything in particular, our training app *will* serve as a reference and a place for experimenting.

Let's write some code.

A Simple App

As I said in Chapter 1, when developing with Rails, you'll be spending a lot of time on the command line. Now is the time to start getting used to that, so fire up the terminal!

I suggest that you create a new folder in your home directory for storing all your Rails projects. I call mine **rails_projects**. Not the most imaginative title, perhaps, but, for the purposes of this book, it would be useful if you follow my example and give yours the same name, then we'll all know where we are.

In terminal, change directory into your **rails_projects** folder:

```
cd ~/rails_projects
```

In Chapter 1, we installed Ruby Version Manager (RVM). One of the many excellent features of RVM is that we can create project specific gemsets. That means we create a bundle of gems dedicated to the project we are working on. If it helps, think of it as a way to manage app-specific dependencies.

Type the following via terminal:

```
rvm use --create 2.0.0@training
```

This creates a new gemset. Next, we install Rails into the new gemset.

```
gem install rails
```

You will now see a ton of text on the screen as all the dependencies of Rails are installed.

Then, to create a Rails app we enter:

```
rails new training
```

Next, we switch into the **training** directory, and create a RVM project file:

```
cd training
rvm --rvmrc 2.0.0@training
```

That's it. We now have a project-specific gemset. The `rails new` command will have generated a whole bunch of files and folders, as seen in Figure 2.1.

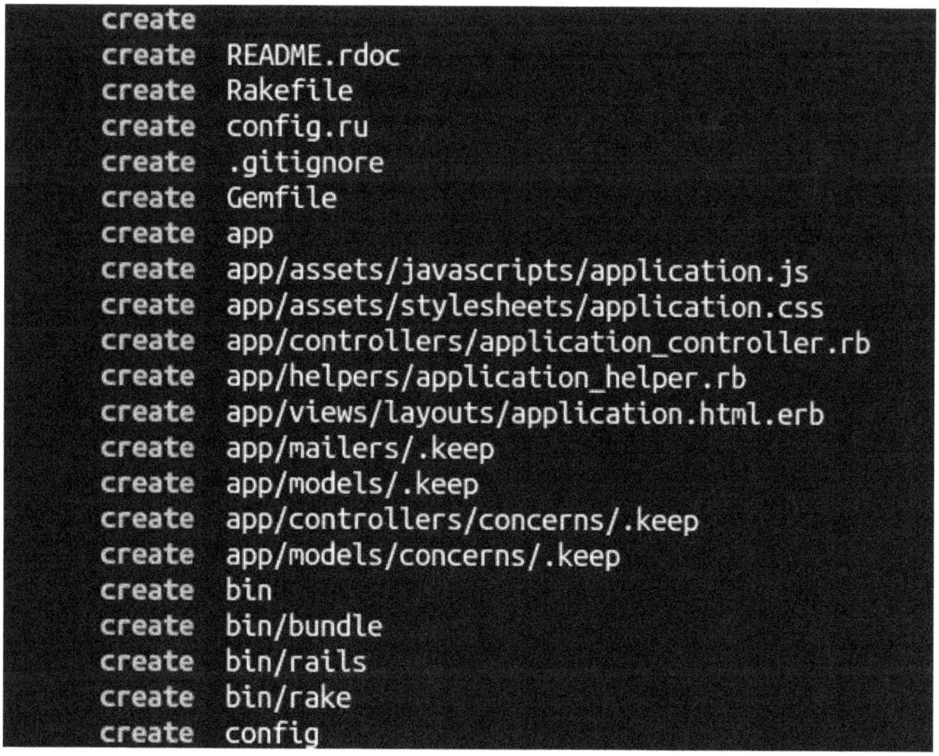

```
      create
      create  README.rdoc
      create  Rakefile
      create  config.ru
      create  .gitignore
      create  Gemfile
      create  app
      create  app/assets/javascripts/application.js
      create  app/assets/stylesheets/application.css
      create  app/controllers/application_controller.rb
      create  app/helpers/application_helper.rb
      create  app/views/layouts/application.html.erb
      create  app/mailers/.keep
      create  app/models/.keep
      create  app/controllers/concerns/.keep
      create  app/models/concerns/.keep
      create  bin
      create  bin/bundle
      create  bin/rails
      create  bin/rake
      create  config
```

Figure 2.1. Generating a new app

As you may have gathered, the `rails new` command has a number of other options you can use. We'll be discovering these as we progress. One such option is to choose which database we want to employ. Since we didn't specify a database in this instance, we'll receive a default SQLite database to use should we need it.

I bet you'd like to see what this app looks like, wouldn't you? Let's take a peek. Back in terminal type:

```
rails server
```

You can shorten that command to just `rails s`. You'll see the built-in server start up, as shown in Figure 2.2.

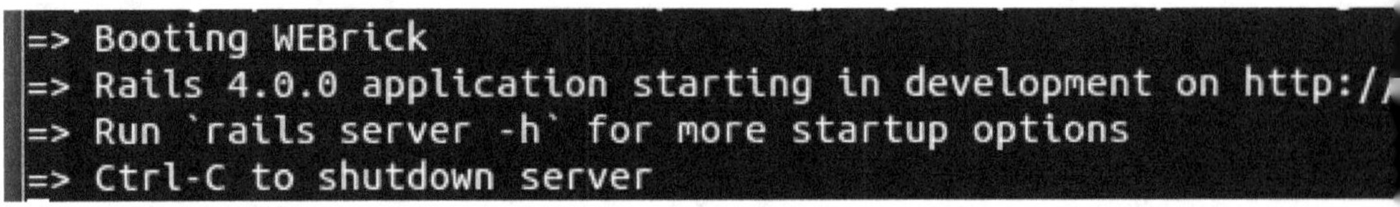

```
=> Booting WEBrick
=> Rails 4.0.0 application starting in development on http://
=> Run `rails server -h` for more startup options
=> Ctrl-C to shutdown server
```

Figure 2.2. Webrick start-up

Should you get an error like "Could not find a JavaScript runtime," then you need to open your Gemfile in an editor and find the line that references "therubyracer". Uncomment this line, save the Gemfile, and type `bundle install` in the terminal. This will create a JavaScript runtime that is used by Rails to evaluate CoffeeScript.

Now you can open your browser, and head to the default Rails welcome page[1], which is shown in Figure 2.3.

[1] http://localhost:3000

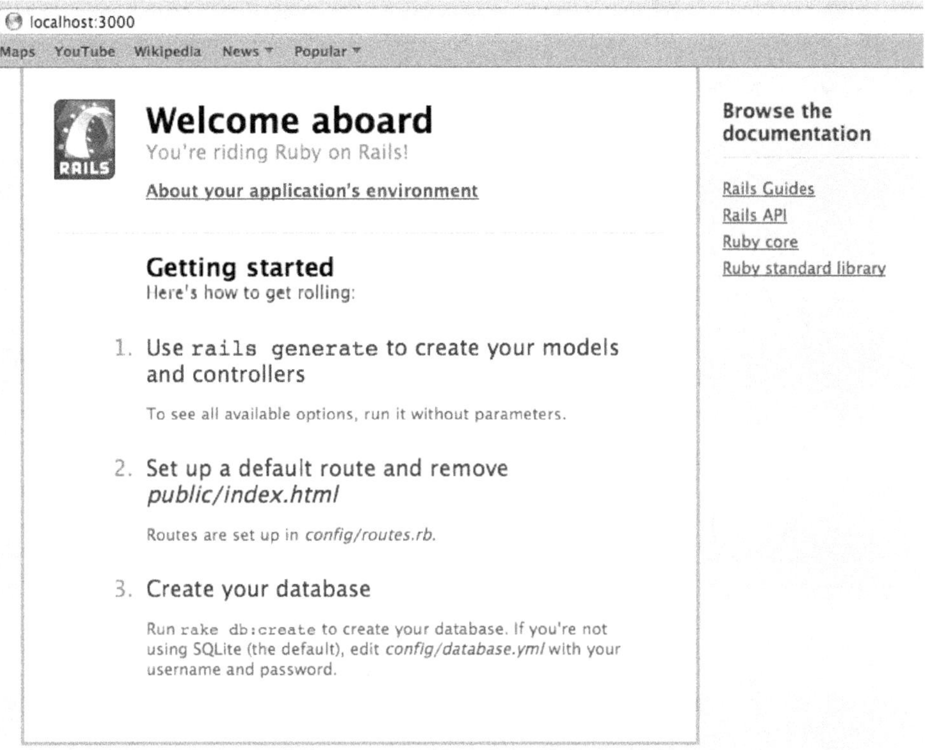

Figure 2.3. Default Rails

Cool! So now you're up and running. However, while the default Rails page is really nice, it would be good if we could create something ourselves. Just before we do that, though, it's worth taking a quick look at all the stuff Rails created for us when we created our app.

The Project Folders

Rails generated a number of folders and files for us, shown in Figure 2.3.

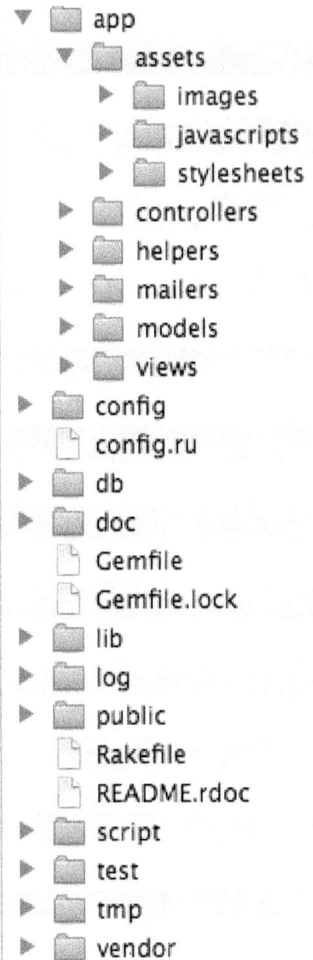

Figure 2.4. A Rails project

Here's a quick run-through of what they all are:

- **app** —The core of your application is found here. This is where you'll spend most of your time.
- **bin** — Rails places any executables associated with your application in this directory. By default, it has the `bundle`, `rails`, and `rake` commands. Yes, this is the same `rails` command you used earlier to start the application server.

- **config** —As the name implies, all the configuration options for your app can be found here, including the `.yml` file for database connection parameters, and `routes.rb` for creating routing options.
- **db** — This is the home for scripts that are used to manage relational database tables.
- **lib** — This is the place for code that isn't a natural fit for model, views, or controllers. You'll put code here that you want to share across resources.
- **log** — Log data about how your app runs is stored here. It doesn't just contain errors, but also information about requests and how they were processed.
- **public** — You'll find the home for default 404 pages, and static HTML files here. In previous versions of Rails, you'd find the default `index.html` here.
- **test** — Rails generates tests for you, and then you add to them to test your application.
- **tmp** — This is where you'll find cached data, temporary files, and session files.
- **vendor** — Third-party code and assets go in this directory.

There are also some other files, such as **Gemfile** and **Gemfile.lock**, but we'll get to those later.

Generators

Generators are the built-in way we generate all sorts of resources for our app. In terminal we can produce a list of the generators we have available to us:

```
rails generate
```

You'll see a list that looks like Figure 2.3.

```
Please choose a generator below.

Rails:
  assets
  controller
  generator
  helper
  integration_test
  jbuilder
  jbuilder_scaffold_controller
  mailer
  migration
  model
  resource
  scaffold
  scaffold_controller
  task

Coffee:
  coffee:assets

Jquery:
  jquery:install

Js:
  js:assets

TestUnit:
  test_unit:plugin
```

Figure 2.5. Rails generators

As we build our app(s) you'll see most of these generators in action.

Generating a Controller

Right now we want to create the simplest page possible, so we need a controller. The function of a controller is to translate an incoming request into an action provided by your application.

Here we go. Back in terminal, enter:

```
rails generate controller pages index about
```

You'll see Rails create the controller for you, as shown in Figure 2.3.

```
      create  app/controllers/pages_controller.rb
       route  get "pages/about"
       route  get "pages/index"
      invoke  erb
      create    app/views/pages
      create    app/views/pages/index.html.erb
      create    app/views/pages/about.html.erb
      invoke  test_unit
      create    test/functional/pages_controller_test.rb
      invoke  helper
      create    app/helpers/pages_helper.rb
      invoke    test_unit
      create      test/unit/helpers/pages_helper_test.rb
      invoke  assets
      invoke    coffee
      create      app/assets/javascripts/pages.js.coffee
      invoke    scss
      create      app/assets/stylesheets/pages.css.scss
```

Figure 2.6. Generating a controller

You'll notice that a bunch of other files are created too. Don't concern yourself with these for now. Instead, let's take a look at the core files Rails generated for us (Figure 2.7).

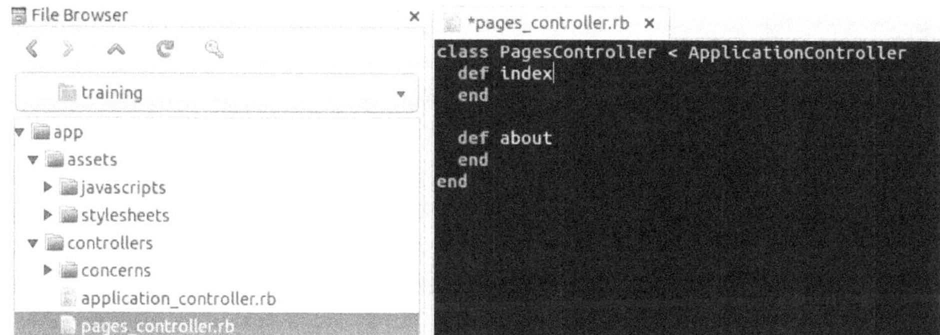

Figure 2.7. The pages_controller

The `rails generate controller` command created the `PagesController` with the two methods we specified: `index` and `about`.

We'll be flipping between terminal and our editor a lot, so it's worth opening another tab in terminal. This way we'll have a tab for typing commands, and a tab for running the Rails server.

Let's test what we've got so far by opening a new tab in terminal and entering: `rails server` or `rails s` for short. Then you can go to `localhost:3000`. Figure 2.8 shows the modest masterpiece you'll be presented with

Figure 2.8. A first look

If we want to spice up our page just a little bit, we can add an **instance variable**, and then display the contents in our view.

In **pages_controller.rb** inside the `index` action, you can add an instance variable, like so:

```
def index
  @notice = "This came from the pages controller"
end
```

Then, in **app/views/pages** we can edit **index.html.erb** like this:

```
<h1>Pages#index</h1>
<p>Find me in app/views/pages/index.html.erb</p>
<p><%= @notice %></p>
```

Figure 2.9. A first change

You may be thinking that, so far, we've put in a lot of effort to display a very simple HTML page. While that's true, you've seen a small piece of Ruby code for the first time. And it provides a glimpse of the power we have to create all sorts of data interactions between our business logic and the user interface. Our `pages` controller has a method called `index` that will render the view called **index.html.erb** in the `views/pages` directory. Hopefully, you can see the conventions of Rails start to become clearer.

In our view, you'll see that Rails replaces the contents of `<%= %>` with the actual value of the instance variable we created in the controller method. In this case, we only sent through a simple string. We can use the same idea for more powerful options though, as we'll see later.

Some Notes About the Controller

Before moving on, we should take a slightly closer look at what happened when we ran the generator. You can see that Rails created a file called **pages_controller.rb**, and inside it we see that there is a class called `PagesController`. So what Rails did was take the name we entered in the generator, and use it to create the resource we requested.

Controllers we generate almost always inherit from the `ApplicationController` class, which is what is meant by the line:

```
class PagesController < ApplicationController
```

The `ApplicationController` is created when we run `rails new`. It can be found in **app/controllers/application_controller.rb**.

We define methods using `def` , so `def index` is the start of our index method. At the moment, we have very little else in the method, so it has `end` pretty much straight away.

Layouts

We can see already that what's presented to us in the browser is a little bland. Part of the fix for this is layouts. They provide a way for us to set out our pages with all the common elements in place, using placeholders for the content that varies for each page.

And in case you're wondering, you can use more than one layout, too.

If you look at the code in our Rails-generated views, you'll notice that they don't even have a full HTML page. Yet if you "view source" in your browser, you'll see complete HTML page code. You might conclude that a layout of some kind is already in use, and you'd be correct. You'll find it in: **app/views/layouts** and it's called **application.html.erb**. This one looks after the whole app. But what if you wanted a layout for a particular controller?

No problem. All you need to do is create a layout file that has the same name as one of your controllers. So, if we create **pages.html.erb** in **app/views/layouts** and add the code below we create something known as a **code spike**. This means it's proof-of-concept code. We'll learn more about code spikes later on in this chapter.

```
<!DOCTYPE html>
<html>
<head>
    <title>Training</title>
    <%= stylesheet_link_tag    "application", :media => "all",
➥"data-turbolinks-track" => true %>
    <%= javascript_include_tag "application", "data-turbolinks-
➥track" => true %>
    <%= csrf_meta_tags %>
</head>
<body>
        <div style="width: 950px; margin: 0px auto;">
            <h2>This is the layout for the pages controller</h2>
            <%= yield %>
        </div>
</body>
</html>
```

You've probably guessed that `<%= yield %>` gets replaced with the contents of the view that we load from the controller action.

If you reload `http://localhost:3000/pages/index` in your browser, you'll see our new layout take effect immediately.

Template Data

There's another neat trick you can use, too. Let's say there's an element of design you want to appear on all pages, but not necessarily with the same content each time. You can add something like this to the `pages` layout:

```
<%= yield :note %>
```

Then, in your views, enter the following:

```
<% content_for(:note) do %>
    <p>This could be different for each view.</p>
<% end %>
```

This is a simple and handy way to work with template data.

Setting the Default Page

Pointing your browser at `http://localhost:3000/pages/index` will deliver the default Ruby on Rails start page. It's fine, but we probably don't want that for our application. This means it's time to do some initial work with Rails routes.

It'd be easy to dedicate an entire book to the wonders of routing with Rails. For now, though, we just need to get something up and running.

If you open **config/routes.rb** you'll see something like this:

```
Training::Application.routes.draw do
    get "pages/index"
    get "pages/about"
```

Rails has already created two routes for the methods we have in our page controller (the generator did that for us). You may be wondering if there's a better way of telling Rails about our `Pages` resource. There is, and we'll get to that a little later. To begin with we'll concentrate on creating simple routes.

To set the default page, in `config/routes.rb` add:

```
root :to => 'pages#index'
```

When you go to `http://localhost:3000/pages/index` now, you should see the page we have been working on.

Creating a Route

You've already seen how a Rails generator created routes for each action in our `pages` controller. That gives us a URL like `http://localhost/pages/about`. What about if we wanted to drop the `pages` part of that URL, though?

Update your routes file (**config/routes.rb**) so it looks like this:

```
Training::Application.routes.draw do
    get "pages/index"
    get "about", :to => 'pages#about'
```

```
    root :to => 'pages#index'
end
```

Then, back in your browser, you can try opening `localhost:3000/about`. You should see that the `about` page is loaded. But what would happen if we wanted a bunch of static pages? Our route file could start getting quite long. This is Rails, however, so there is a better way.

Ryan Bates of railscasts.com[2] fame has a useful solution[3] for this. All we need to do is create an array in the routes file, then we can pass in a variable to process the actual route for us, like this:

routes.rb (excerpt)

```
Training::Application.routes.draw do
    root :to => 'pages#index'

    %w[about contact cv].each do |page|
      get page, controller: 'pages', action: page
    end
end
```

The `%w[...` element is Ruby shorthand for creating an array from strings without having to quote each string. It saves typing all those commas; for example: `values = ["one", "two", "five", "three sir", "three"]`

After you have created the actions and views, visiting `localhost:3000/contact` will display your `contact` page. Notice that our array has also eliminated the need for `pages` to be in our URLs too. How great is that?

Some Linking

We can link our two views together using the `link_to` method. For example, in **app/views/pages/index.html.erb** you can add:

---

[2] http://www.railscasts.com

[3] http://railscasts.com/episodes/117-semi-static-pages-revised

```
<p><%= link_to "About", '/about' %></p>
```

In the generated source in your browser, you'll see this:

```
<p><a href="/about">About</a></p>
```

Then, in `app/views/about.html.erb` you can add:

```
<p><%= link_to "Home", '/' %></p>
```

It's basic, but at least you've seen how we can link our static pages.

Some Styling

So, we can create layouts, and we can do some basic routing, but our pages still look ugly. Let's do something about that next.

It's worth noting that stylesheets in Rails use Sass[4]. Sass became part of Rails at version 3.1 and is described as a "meta-language on top of CSS." It provides more control over styling by adding features such as nested rules, variables, mixins and more. Variables, for example, are a useful feature of Sass; imagine needing to assign a colour to multiple elements in your stylesheet. With a Sass variable you only have to do it once.

Also, remember when we generated the controller and Rails generated a bunch of other files for us? Well, one of those other files was a stylesheet for our pages controller.

Take a look in **app/assets/stylesheets** and you'll see a file called: **pages.css.scss**. For now, any style rules that we want to apply to our pages controller can go in there. Let's add some:

[4] http://sass-lang.com/

pages.css.scss (excerpt)

```
body{
    font-family: Georgia, Times, "Times New Roman", serif;
    font-size: 1.2em;
}
```

You can check your changes in the browser, or add more styles if you wish. You may be wondering how the style rule(s) you added got picked up by Rails.

If you remember, in the layout file (**app/views/layouts/pages.html.erb**) there is a line of code that looks like this:

```
<%= stylesheet_link_tag    "application", media:"all", "data-turbolinks-track"
```

Any style rules that you add to your stylesheets are compiled and included in **application.css** at run time. Neat, eh?

Putting up Some Scaffolding

We now have a simple app that responds to requests for static pages. We'll use this knowledge for our personal website's info pages. A simple blog engine is also one of the features for our main app. While we're working with the training app, it's worth taking a look at a feature in Rails called **scaffolding**.

Scaffolding lets you quickly create a resource that interacts with the database. You pass in the field names that you want, and Rails pretty much does the rest. It can be useful for creating a working version of a particular feature in a single operation. It's also useful for getting an overview of working with data in a Rails app.

We don't employ scaffolding like this in a production app. This is largely because the end goals are more complex than scaffolding is able to produce. But while, usually, it's easier just to write Rails code in the first place, it *is* worth a look.

Generating a Scaffold

In terminal, make sure you are in your project folder. Then enter:

```
rails g scaffold Post title:string blurb:string body:text
```

You'll see that a bunch of files are created, shown in Figure 2.10.

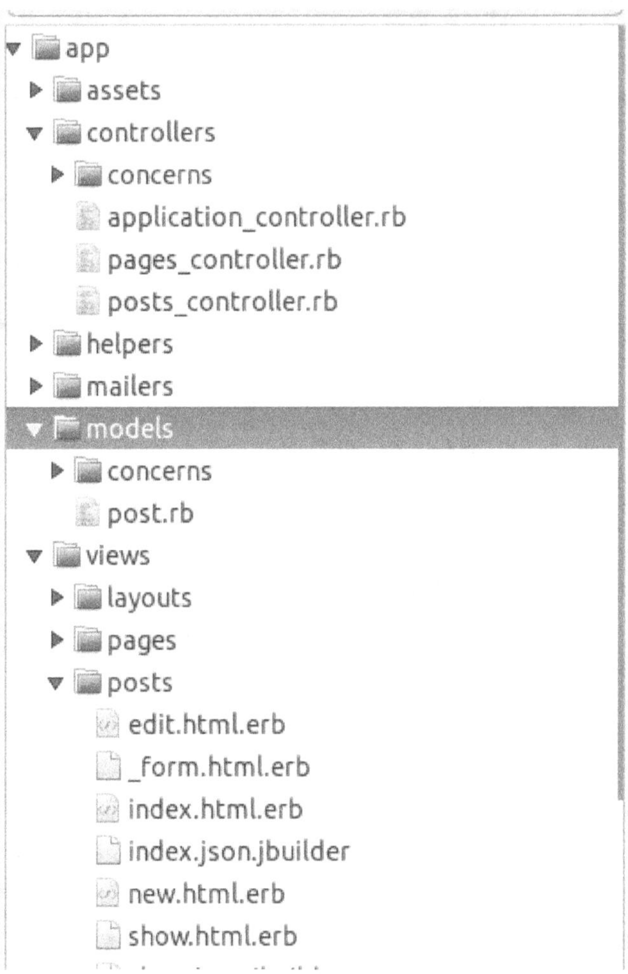

Figure 2.10. Rails scaffolding

You can see that Rails created a controller, model, and an assortment of views. You'll notice that Rails added `resources :posts` to your **routes.rb** file too.

The next thing we have to do is migrate the database. Migrations let you alter your database in a structured and organized way, saving you the chore of editing SQL by hand.

To achieve this we use our friend rake, like so:

```
rake db:migrate
```

`rake`, also called "ruby make," is a build program that allows you to create and run tasks easily. Rails uses rake for many things.

The above command will run any outstanding migrations. Rails is clever enough to figure out which migrations have already been processed. We didn't specify a database, so Rails will use a default SQLite database. Figure 2.11 shows what's generated (in the **db** directory):

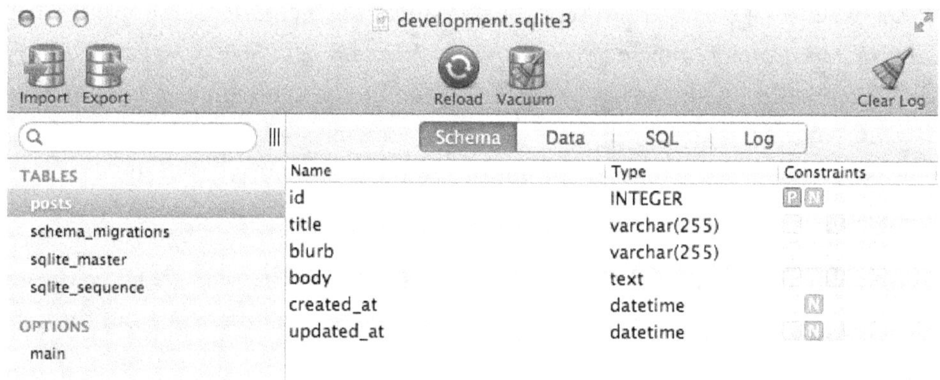

Figure 2.11. Rails database

We can see that Rails chose SQLite by taking a look at the **/config/database.yml** file:

database.yml

```
# SQLite version 3.x
#   gem install sqlite3
#
#   Ensure the SQLite 3 gem is defined in your Gemfile
#   gem 'sqlite3'
development:
  adapter: sqlite3
  database: db/development.sqlite3
  pool: 5
  timeout: 5000

# Warning: The database defined as "test" will be erased and
# re-generated from your development database when you run "rake".
```

```
# Do not set this db to the same as development or production.
test:
  adapter: sqlite3
  database: db/test.sqlite3
  pool: 5
  timeout: 5000

production:
  adapter: sqlite3
  database: db/production.sqlite3
  pool: 5
  timeout: 5000
```

So now we have a basic structure for the sample blog element of our app. You can visit your creation by pointing your browser at `localhost:3000/posts`. There, you will be greeted by an empty list of posts. We can fix that, though. Click the **Add Post** link, and you'll be taken through to a form. Enter a couple of posts using this, and you'll see that when the form is submitted, you are now populating the database.

After you have submitted a post, clicking the **Back** link will take you back to the listing of all your posts. Click the **Edit** link next to the post, and you get taken through to a form where you can change any part of the contents of the post, and then re-save it.

Likewise, if you click on the **Delete** link, you will be prompted first, as shown in Figure 2.12.

Figure 2.12. Deleting a post

Click **OK** and the post will be deleted.

What we have here is a working application. It's a long way from being complete, of course, but it does give a useful insight into what can be achieved. There are some issues to address, though. For example, we wouldn't want our blog admin to be available to everyone, would we? And what happens if we try adding an empty record? Give it a go.

Fixing the permissions/authentication problem is a bigger deal, so we'll come to that a little later. However, fixing the empty record problem can be achieved quickly, so let's do that now.

To begin with, let's make sure we understand what happens when we are working with records via the forms that scaffolding produced for us.

Open up **app/controllers/post_controller.rb** and you'll see that we have actions named: `index`, `show`, `new`, `edit`, `create`, `update`, and `delete`. Each of these is designed to respond to an HTTP verb (POST, GET, DELETE, etc.).

The `index` action contains an ActiveRecord call: `@posts = Post.all` to retrieve all the records in the `posts` table in our database.

The `show` action retrieves one record using the passed-in parameter of the post id your user clicked on: `@post = Post.find(params[:id])`.

The `new` action provides a form for users to add a new record to the database. The call to `Post.new` creates a new blank structure based on the `Post` model. The controller doesn't worry about what the actual schema for a post is; it just passes the structure to the view. It's the `create` method that performs the actual save to the database.

The `edit` action also uses GET to collect a record for user editing: `@post = Post.find(params[:id])`. The record is passed to the view that contains a form that you then use to make the edits. Like `new`, the actual data editing doesn't take place here. The changes will be processed via the `update` method.

The `create` method creates a new `Post` object based on the `:post` parameters sent in from the form. You'll see in the `create` action that an attempt is made to save the data with `if @post.save`. If the attempt is successful, the user is informed that the save succeeded. If it fails, the error is reported back to the user and the incoming data is sent to a copy of the form with:

```
else
    format.html { render action: "new" }
```

The `update` action works much the same way as `create`, but it responds to PUT rather than POST. The record to update is selected via the passed-in parameter from the URL: `@post = Post.find(params[:id])`. Once the record is found, the `update_attributes` method is used to try to change the stored values. There is a success or error response here too.

The `delete` action responds to the HTTP DELETE request. Again, the record for deletion is selected via the passed-in parameter. There are two things that happen. First, the object is located and then a call to the DESTROY method is made. It is assumed that the delete process has happened, so there is a redirect to the main list of posts. The form contains some JavaScript to get the user to confirm that they want to delete the record. Notice that the action doesn't have anything to request that the user confirm the deletion.

Finally, you may be wondering why a few of our actions mention format and what this means. Briefly, Rails controllers respond to requests for HTML pages by default, so when you go to `localhost:300/posts`, you get an HTML representation of the existing posts. You don't have to say you want HTML, because it is the default presentation mode, but you could if you appended `.html` to your request like so: `http://localhost:3000/posts.html`. Rails controllers can also respond to requests for JavaScript Object Notation (JSON). JSON is a serializable, text-based format that is readily consumed by JavaScript clients, like your web browser. JSON is most often used to create Application Programming Interfaces (APIs) and is not meant to be seen by humans. I won't be covering JSON and API creation in this book, but your career as a Rails developer will, no doubt, take you down that path eventually.

Active Record Validations

Let's face it — people don't always enter the data we'd like them to enter. Even *you* might be guilty of this occasionally — when entering a new blog post on your own blog, for example. And because we live in an imperfect world we need some way of protecting our data integrity.

One thing we can do straight away is to add some validation to strengthen our models. By adding a few simple rules to our models, we can automatically have Rails do the heavy lifting for us. By default we add validation rules to our models, and Rails then applies the rules to our forms, including a nice notification system, shown in Figure 2.13.

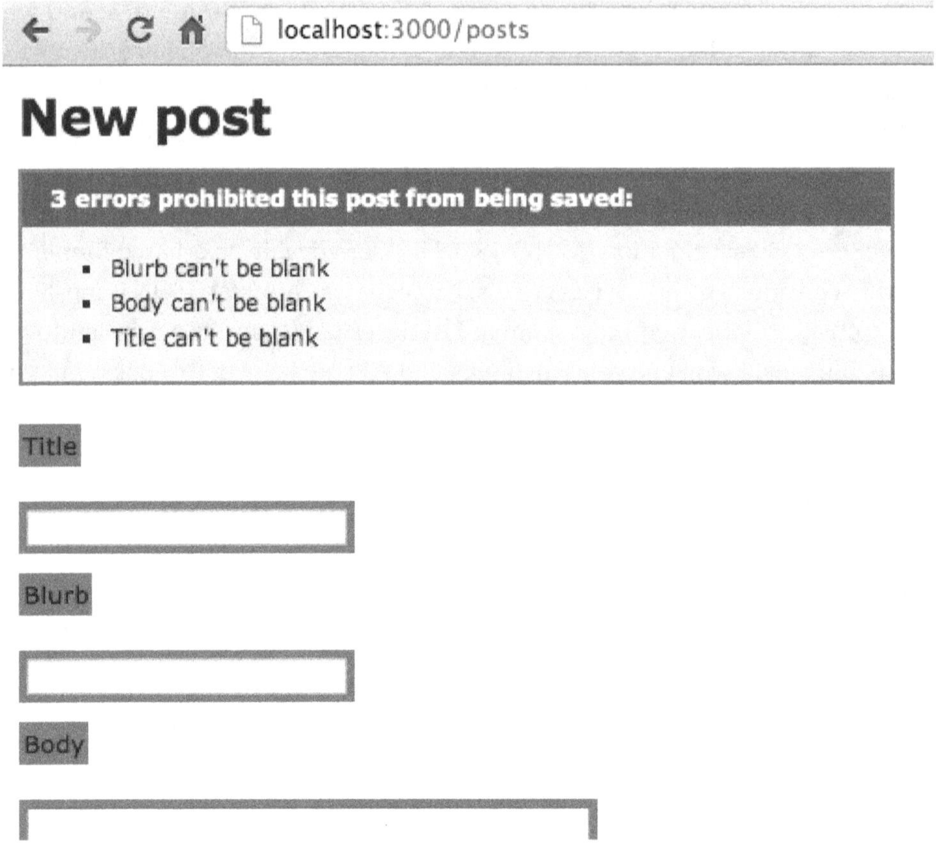

Figure 2.13. Rails validation

And that's that, for basic validation anyway. Let's take a closer look, though; what does the actual code in the model look like?

```
class Post < ActiveRecord::Base
  attr_accessible :title, :slug, :blurb, :content
  validates :body, :title, :presence => true
end
```

You should try each of the following in your browser, so that you can see how Rails handles each validation change. You'll be impressed, I promise.

Here, we're using `validates_presence_of` to ensure that a value is added for each field. It's the least we can do to protect our models. What happens, though, when we have a text field that should contain a certain amount of text? For example, it seems reasonable that our blurb field should contain at least 10 characters. We can validate for that:

```
class Post < ActiveRecord::Base
  attr_accessible :title, :slug, :blurb, :content
  validates :blurb, :length => { :minimum => 10 }
  validates :body, :title, :presence => true
end
```

There is something else we can do to strengthen the validation on the blurb field. Since the field has the data type of `string`, it's limited in capacity to around 255 characters. So let's create a validation rule that satisfies both conditions (minimum and maximum):

```
class Post < ActiveRecord::Base
  validates :blurb, :length => { :in => 10..255 }
  validates :body, :title, :presence => true
end
```

Here, you can see that the number of characters is restricted within acceptable parameters for our database table. There's one more thing. What about a situation in which we only want text to be added? That is, characters, not numbers? We can do that, too, by adding a regular expression:

```
validates :blurb, :length => { :in => 10..255 }, :format => { :with
➥=> /^\A[a-zA-Z\d ]+\z/, :message => "Only letters allowed",
➥:multiline => true}
```

Now we have validation that works in the way we want.

Test Driven Development

The first thing to note is that Rails was built with testing in mind. You'll have already spotted that tests are generated for you each time you add a new resource.

The second thing is that Rails has its testing rig built-in. You can use others, such as RSpec[5]. In truth, you may find that you switch to RSpec quite quickly because of its support for Behavior Driven Development (BDD).

---

[5] http://rspec.info/

We'll focus on Ruby's built-in Test::Unit here, though. It has plenty to offer and provides good code coverage for our app.

You can think of TDD as a design activity. It furthers the purpose of testing from being just a way to make sure code runs as expected. Rather, TDD offers a way to clarify the purpose of the code. As you add new features to your app, you create tests that test the idea with which you're working.

If you're new to TDD, Figure 2.14 shows a diagram that explains the basic concept behind it.

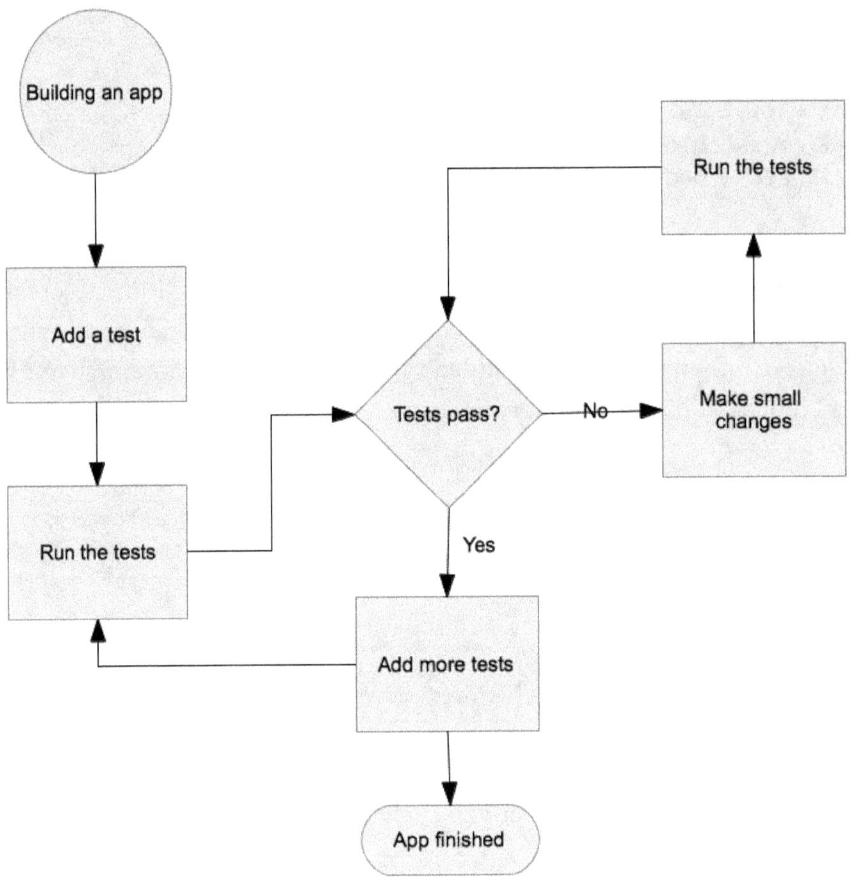

Figure 2.14. Test Driven Development

It also means that we need to know what we are testing for. So when you're adding a new test, you'll already need to know what you expect to happen. You might figure that out by writing a code spike. All that means is code that won't make it into production, but which enables you to figure out what you're attempting to do.

The tests you create, then, help to steer the design of the app based on the required functionality. By writing your tests first, they will fail initially. But as you figure out the design, you will eventually receive passing tests. From here you tighten up the code to make it as good as it can be. This process is often referred to as "red, green, refactor."

Let's see what Rails has to offer.

The Environments

All Rails applications have three environments: one for production, one for development, and one for testing. If you take a look in your **config/database.yml** file, you'll see the three environments clearly. The test database is designed to be used for all your testing activity. As such, it shouldn't matter if you end up deleting its data.

You can make sure that the test database is ready to go with:

```
rake db:test:prepare
```

This ensures that there are no pending migrations. And it loads the test schema for the database.

Tests Rails Has Already Generated

Figure 2.15 shows the tests Rails has already generated.

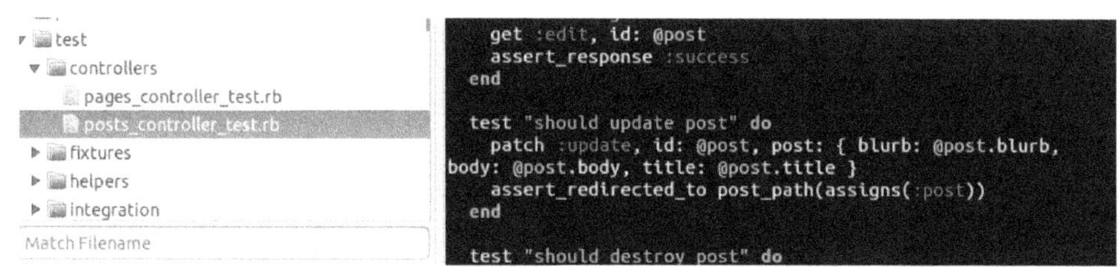

Figure 2.15. Rails tests

What we have here is a **models** folder for testing models, a **controllers** folder for testing controllers, and an **integration** folder for tests that involve controllers interacting. You'll notice that we also have a **fixtures** folder. Fixtures is just another way of saying sample data.

Fixtures

Good tests require good fixtures. Rails will populate your test database with predefined data before the tests are run. They are created using the YAML format. As you begin to create resources, Rails will generate some fixtures for you. Take a look in **test/fixtures**:

```
one:
  title: MyString
  blurb: MyString
  body: MyText

two:
  title: MyString
  blurb: MyString
  body: MyText
```

You probably should replace the content with something more meaningful for our application:

posts.yml

```
one:
  title: The first post
  blurb: This post won't be about very much at all.
  body: So, here is a meaningless post.

two:
  title: The second post
  blurb: There had to be two, didn't there?
  body: Yep, you guessed it, this is the second post.
```

Rails will automatically load the fixtures found in **test/fixtures** for the unit and functional tests that you create.

Something to Watch Out For

Fixtures can make your tests brittle. The reason, simply, is this: you create fixtures for one set of tests, and they pass. But then you change the fixtures for another test or tests and, while those tests might pass, the fixture change can then break the original tests.

There is an answer, though, which we'll see in action shortly. In short, it revolves around specifying which fixture file gets loaded for our tests. After all, the default action by Rails is to load *all* the fixtures, because, to Rails, it seems logical that's what you'd want. For now, just keep in mind that there's a way to get past the problem should you need to.

Unit Testing Models

I mentioned earlier that Unit Tests are tests for your models. The default test (in **test/models/post_test.rb**) that Rails has created for us when we created the `posts` scaffold looks like this:

```
require 'test_helper'

class PostTest < ActiveSupport::TestCase
  # test "the truth" do
  #   assert true
  # end
end
```

The **test_helper** file contains the default configuration used to run our tests. You can see that our testing class inherits from: `ActiveSupport::TestCase`.

Let's run a test. We'll need to make sure everything is ready to go with:

```
rake db:migrate
rake db:test:load
```

Looking at the code in our test, we can uncomment the `the truth` method, and then from the terminal enter:

```
rake test
```

You should get something like Figure 2.16.

```
Run options: --seed 41966

# Running tests:

.........

Finished tests in 0.574455s, 15.6670 tests/s, 26.1117 assertions/s.

9 tests, 15 assertions, 0 failures, 0 errors, 0 skips
```

Figure 2.16. A first test

The '.' indicates a passing test. We've used a simple truth **assertion** here. Assertions are used to evaluate an object or expression for the expected results. Obviously this is not a test of our app, but it demonstrates how to run a test. It's worth noting that `Test::Unit` comes with some ready-to-run tests.

If your tests fail, it's likely due to the validators we added on the `Post` model above. Can you get them to pass? If not, don't worry, we'll get them to pass in a bit.

Now we'll add an actual test. Here, we want to make sure that when a post is saved it has a title. You may remember that we have a validation that already does this. But let's create the test anyway:

```
test "should not save post without title" do
    post = Post.new
    assert !post.save
end
```

Now, when we run `rake test`, what happens? That's right: all our tests and assertions pass. If you temporarily comment out the validations in **app/models/post.rb**, however, and run the test again you'll see your first failing test.

Now, if you're thinking that there's no point testing when you can use validations, not so fast. Think about what we've done here: if we were using proper TDD techniques, we'd have written our test *before* adding any validation. Unit tests on models are mostly for ensuring that we're getting the data we want. So our test proves that we have a fighting chance of getting the data we want in our database.

There are still more improvements that can be made. For example, how can we test those validations? It'd be nice if we could actually test that the validations do what we think they are going to do. Well, guess what? This is Rails, so we can do just that.

Here's a new test to add to **test/unit/post_test.rb**:

```
test "post values should not be empty" do
    post = Post.new
    assert post.invalid?
    assert post.errors[:title].any?
    assert post.errors[:blurb].any?
    assert post.errors[:body].any?
end
```

Can you see how this addresses the issue about tests versus validations? This test creates a new post, fires it at the model, and then ensures that the model correctly fires errors back because the fields can't be blank. How awesome is that? You can run the tests with `rake test:units`, too.

This means we know that the model is working in its most basic form. We can now drill down and do some specific testing. For example, our validations say that the blurb field should only accept text. Let's make sure that's going to be the case. And while we're at it, we'll use one of our fixtures to throw some data at the test too:

```
test "blurb should be a string" do
    post = Post.new(title: posts(:one).title,
                    blurb: posts(:one).blurb,
                    body: "Body? Whose?")

    assert blurb.title.kind_of? String
end
```

Run the tests, and we get:

```
Run options:
# Running tests:
..
Finished tests in 0.095570s, 20.9271 tests/s, 52.3177 assertions/s.
2 tests, 5 assertions, 0 failures, 0 errors, 0 skips
```

The line that's interesting here is: `blurb: posts(:one).blurb`. What this does is load the fixture data from **test/fixtures/posts.yml** from the record named `one`. Use descriptive fixture names. "One" is fine for this simple example, but more descriptive names will make things easier in a bigger app.

Functional Tests

We can also test the controllers. Or, to put it another way, test the user-facing layers. Controller tests let us check with assertions how a single request to a controller action is handled. The scaffolding we generated has created a whole series of tests already. Take a look in **test/controllers/posts_controller_test.rb** to see what I mean.

Now run them with: `rake test:functionals`, and you'll notice they fail. Why is that?

When we try to add a blank record, the model validation kicks in, and the tests fail. What we need to do is change the tests in order to reflect that fact.

We do this by setting up the test so that some data actually gets fired at the model. Open up **test/functional/posts_controller_test.rb** and add the setup code like this:

```
class PostsControllerTest < ActionController::TestCase
  setup do
    @post = posts(:one)
    @update = {
      title: 'Here is the title',
      blurb: 'Here is the blurb',
      body: 'Here is the body'
    }
  end
```

The two tests that failed were: `should get new` and `should update post`. For the new post test, update it to look like this:

```
test "should create post" do
    assert_difference('Post.count') do
    post :create, post: @update
end
```

As for the update test, alter the code like this:

```
test "should update post" do
    put :update, id: @post, post: @update
    assert_redirected_to post_path(assigns(:post))
end
```

Done? Now rerun the tests:

```
Run options:
# Running tests:
.........
Finished tests in 0.443877s, 20.2759 tests/s, 27.0345 assertions/s.
9 tests, 12 assertions, 0 failures, 0 errors, 0 skips
```

Excellent. Problem solved! Hopefully this little run-though of writing some tests for our app has shown you the power of Rails' built-in testing.

Creating a Layout with Bootstrap

There are lots of reasons to like the flexibility that offered by Rails layouts. However, if you're not a designer, making something that looks nice can still be a challenge. Enter Bootstrap[6]. Bootstrap is a CSS framework that provides a set of grids for layout, typographical and HTML element styles, and some cool JavaScript interactions.

Thanks to the extensive Ruby ecosystem there are several gems we can use with our Rails app to seamlessly integrate Bootstrap. The example I'll demonstrate here (we'll be using it in our main app, too) is called boostrap sass[7].

It takes very little effort to set the gem up, and it's also very easy to add the Bootstrap resources into our app.

Install the Gem

Open up your Gemfile, and add the line:

```
gem 'bootstrap-sass'
```

Then, in terminal, run `bundle install`.

---

6 http://twitter.github.com/bootstrap/

7 https://github.com/thomas-mcdonald/bootstrap-sass

Connect the Bootstrap Assets

Next, create a new **custom.css.scss** file in **app/assets/stylesheets**. There are other ways to add the Bootstrap styles, but I've found that by having a separate file, it's easy to add the style rules you want to use for the layout, among other things.

To use the Bootstrap stylesheets just add the following to **custom.css.scss**:

```
@import "bootstrap";
@import "bootstrap-responsive";
```

To use the Bootstrap JavaScript files, just add `//= require bootstrap` to **app/assets/javascripts/application.js** like this:

```
//= require jquery
//= require jquery_ujs
//= require_tree .
//= require bootstrap
```

That's it, Bootstrap is now installed.

So now we can start thinking about a layout. The Bootstrap website has some useful examples, so we'll borrow one of those. I've chosen the fluid layout[8] example.

First, let's copy the style rules found in the `<head>` of the example file into our **custom.css.scss** file:

```
body {
    padding-top: 60px;
    padding-bottom: 40px;
}

.sidebar-nav {
    padding: 9px 0;
}
```

Then, copy and paste the HTML code from the sample into your **app/views/layouts/pages.html.erb** file. We're using a fluid layout, meaning that Bootstrap will use percentage values rather than pixels for column widths.

---

[8] http://twitter.github.com/bootstrap/examples/fluid.html

Your layout file should now look like this:

```
<!DOCTYPE html>
<html>
<head>
    <meta name="viewport" content="width=device-width,
➥initial-scale=1.0">
    <%= stylesheet_link_tag    "application", :media => "all",
➥"data-turbolinks-track" => true%>
    <%= javascript_include_tag "application",
➥"data-turbolinks-track" => true %>
    <%= csrf_meta_tags %>
</head>
<body>
  <div class="navbar navbar-inverse navbar-fixed-top">
    <div class="navbar-inner">
      <div class="container-fluid">
         <a class="brand">Jump Start Rails</a>
      </div>
     </div>
  </div>
  <div class="container-fluid">
    <div class="row-fluid">
      <div class="span3">
        <ul class="nav nav-list">
          <li class="nav-header">Sidebar</li>
          <li class="active"><a href="#">Link</a></li>
          <li class="nav-header">Sidebar</li>
          <li><a href="#">Link</a></li>
          <li><a href="#">Link</a></li>
          <li class="nav-header">Sidebar</li>
          <li><a href="#">Link</a></li>
        </ul>
      </div>
      <div class="span9">
        <%= yield %>
      </div>
    </div>
    <hr/>
    <footer></footer>
  </div>

</body>
</html>
```

Refining the Layout

What we have is looking good, but there are still some improvements we can make. For example, it's reasonable to assume that we'll want the menu to appear on most of our pages. So rather than leave that big, untidy blob in the layout file, we'll move it into a **partial**.

You can think of partials as a kind of include file. They are created using the handy `render` method. To create one for the menu, do the following:

Add a new folder in **app/views** called **shared**. Inside that folder, create a file called **_menu.html.erb**. Note the "_". That's how we tell Rails we intend this file to be a partial. You can now copy the code for the left-hand menu into it:

```
<ul class="nav nav-list">
    <li class="nav-header">Sidebar</li>
    <li class="active"><a href="#">Link</a></li>
    <li class="nav-header">Sidebar</li>
    <li><a href="#">Link</a></li>
    <li><a href="#">Link</a></li>
    <li class="nav-header">Sidebar</li>
    <li><a href="#">Link</a></li>
</ul>
```

In **pages.html.erb**, replace the navigation (in the `<div class="span3">` tag) with the following:

```
<%= render "/shared/menu" %>
```

Figure 2.17 shows how it looks by starting the server from terminal, and pointing your browser at `localhost:3000`.

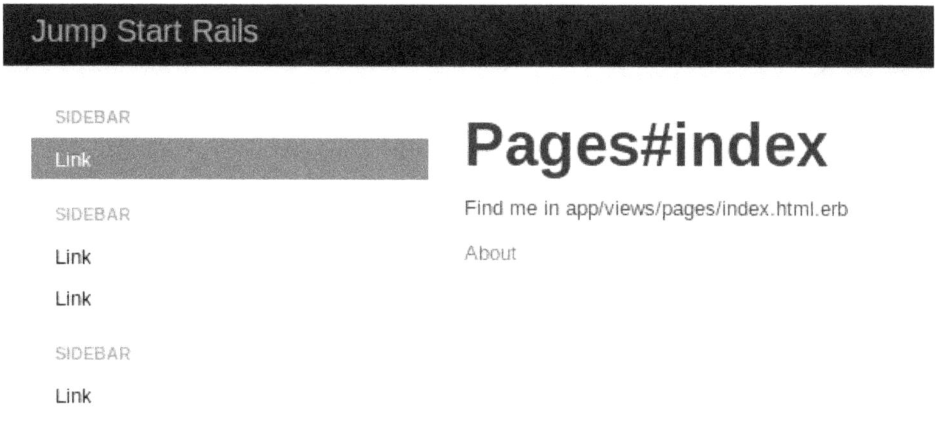

Figure 2.17. Layout with Bootstrap

Some Notes about the Rails Asset Pipeline

It used to be that, when developing a Rails application, anything that was a static resource got thrown into the junk drawer located in the **public** folder. As a result JavaScript, stylesheets, and images were all piled in there with impunity.

At RailsConf 2011 Rails creator David Heinemeier Hansson pointed out the problem, and explained how the assets for an app should be considered part of the app, rather than as stuff thrown in the **public** folder as an afterthought.

That gave rise to the Sprockets library being included in Rails from version 3.1. The library is responsible for compiling and serving static web assets such as JavaScript and CSS files. It can also function as a "preprocessor pipeline," meaning it can use Sass/SCSS as you've already seen.

This compiling can be seen, too. First, run your app as normal, fire up `localhost:3000`, and then do a "view source" in your browser. You will see a long list of stylesheets and JavaScript files listed in the `<head>` section of the document.

Next, stop the server, and restart it with this command (which runs the app in production mode):

```
rails server -e production
```

It's worth noting here, that if you are using a database other than SQLite, you'll need to ensure that you have proper connection parameters set in **config/database.yml**.

When you load the app in your browser, you'll most likely see an unstyled page. If you look in the server log, you'll see something like this:

```
ActionController::RoutingError (No route matches
➥[GET] "/stylesheets/application.css"):
```

What's happening here? Well, the message is telling you to edit: **/config/enviroments/production.rb** and ensure that the `config.assets.compile` is set to `true`. Then re-start the server using `Rails server -e production`, as before. When you refresh your browser, the app should load as normal. Do a "view source," and you'll see that the long list of resources are now only displayed as one file reference.

Pop back into terminal, and you'll see this:

```
I, [2013-05-05T09:00:30.450735 #2688]  INFO -- :
➥Processing by PagesController#index as HTML
I, [2013-05-05T09:00:30.468154 #2688]  INFO -- :
➥Rendered pages/index.html.erb within layouts/pages (1.1ms)
I, [2013-05-05T09:00:49.899789 #2688]  INFO -- :
➥Rendered shared/_menu.html.erb (0.9ms)
...
```

What you can see here is the asset pipeline doing its thing. Our assets have been compiled into single files (one for JavaScript, one for CSS) and are now integrated into the app.

Summary

In this chapter, we've made a simple app by creating a layout and some views first. We've also taken a look at scaffolding to quickly prototype an app and sampled the built-in testing capabilities that Rails has to offer. Lastly, we've seen how we're going to create our layout for the main project app that we'll be building throughout the rest of the book.

In Chapter 3, we'll start developing the main app in earnest and, while we're at it, introduce a site administration system to make it easy to work with the content for our app.

Chapter 3

Working with Data

The focus of this chapter is to begin building our project app in earnest. We'll create resources and see how we can work with migrations to add to, and change, the structure of our database tables. We'll also install a Ruby gem called ActiveAdmin[1] that will give us a really slick interface to manage the database content for our app.

Aside from the fact that ActiveAdmin is a powerful administration tool, it's also a valuable time saver. And since *Jump Start Rails* is a short book, we'll be using it here for that very reason. You should be aware of that, and the fact that ActiveAdmin won't be the right choice for *all* apps you might build. If, for example, you need to design a lot of flexibility into your app, using the application controllers to create an administrative section is the way to go.

The app we'll be building is designed to be a personal web app that includes a blog, a portfolio section, and a mail form, among other things. We'll be deploying it to Heroku[2] once we're done. You may want to add different sections to your app, so we'll be covering enough to give you a platform to do that.

---

[1] http://activeadmin.info

[2] http://www.heroku.com

Lastly, because we're planning to use ActiveAdmin, there's no need for us to create any scaffolding. However, to get the most out of this useful gem, we need to have something up and running first. So let's get coding.

Starting the App

We'll get started with a new project, but this time we'll be using the PostgreSQL database:

```
rails new jumpstartrails -d postgresql
cd jumpstartrails
```

If you created a gemset for your "training" app in the last chapter, you will have to create a new gemset for this app. `rvm use --create 2.0.0@jumpstartrails` followed by `gem install rails` will get your `rails` command back.

We've used the `-d` switch here, to tell Rails that we want to use a different database, PostgreSQL in this case. Rails will use that information to create a different **config/database.yml** file from the one we saw in Chapter 2. We'll be adding our database role credentials in that file shortly.

Switching Rails...

The `rails new` command has a lot of "switches" you can use. For example, you could add `--skip-gemfile` so that Rails doesn't create a Gemfile. You can see all the available options by entering: `rails new -h` in Terminal.

I've stuck with the name `jumpstartrails` but you can (and should) call your app whatever you'd like. You should now change into the **project** directory in terminal.

When you run `rails new` it will create a directory with the same name as the overall project. So, using my example, that would be **jumpstartrails**. You'll need to change into the new directory to continue working on the project.

It's a good idea to create a new role in PostgreSQL for your app. It's simple to do that using the excellent pgAdmin tool, as shown in Figure 3.1.

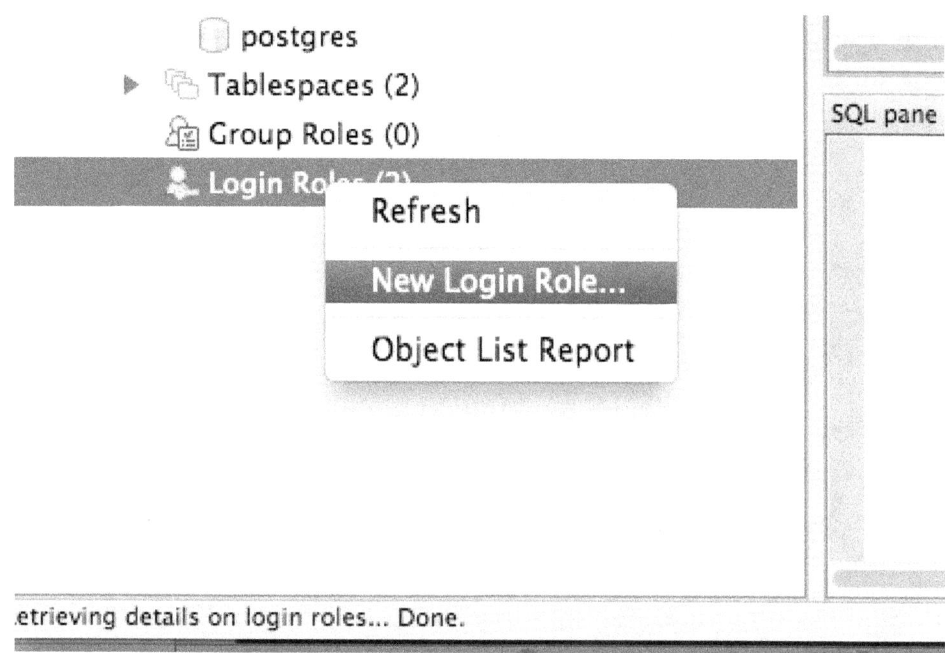

Figure 3.1. pgAdmin roles

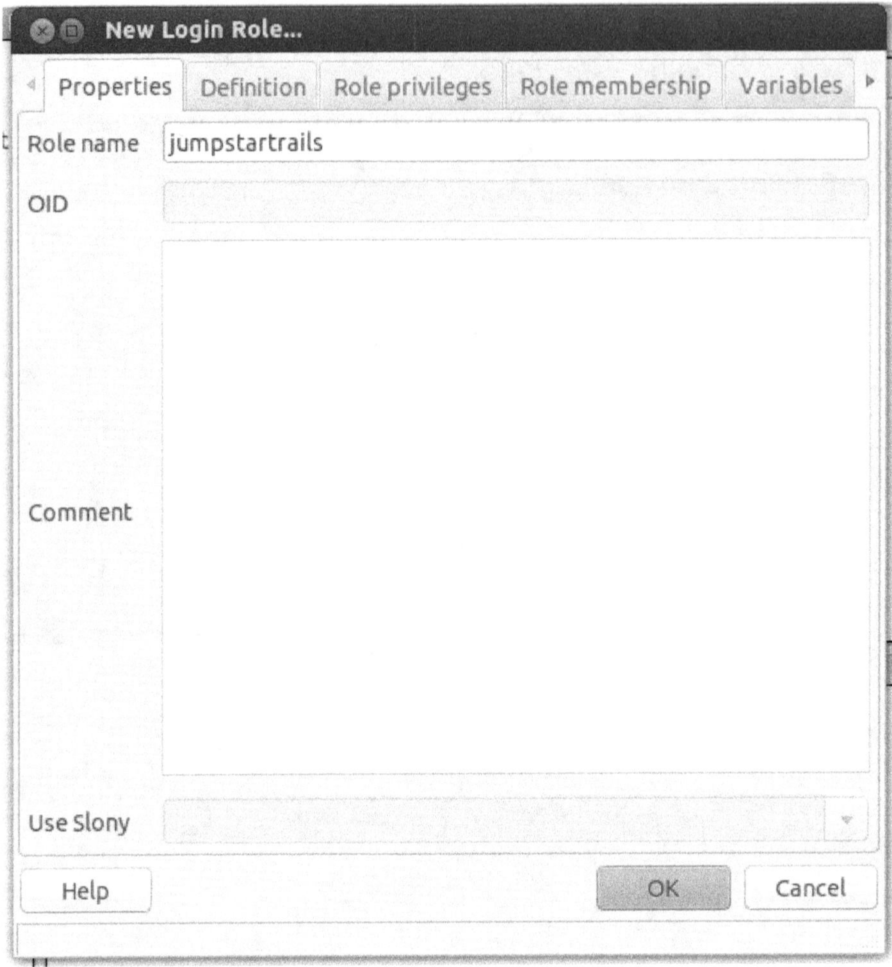

Figure 3.2. New pgAdmin Login role

You'll need to supply a role name ("jumpstartrails" in Figure 3.2) and a password (in the **Definition** tab). The role will also need the ability to create databases (in the **Role privileges** tab, shown in Figure 3.3).

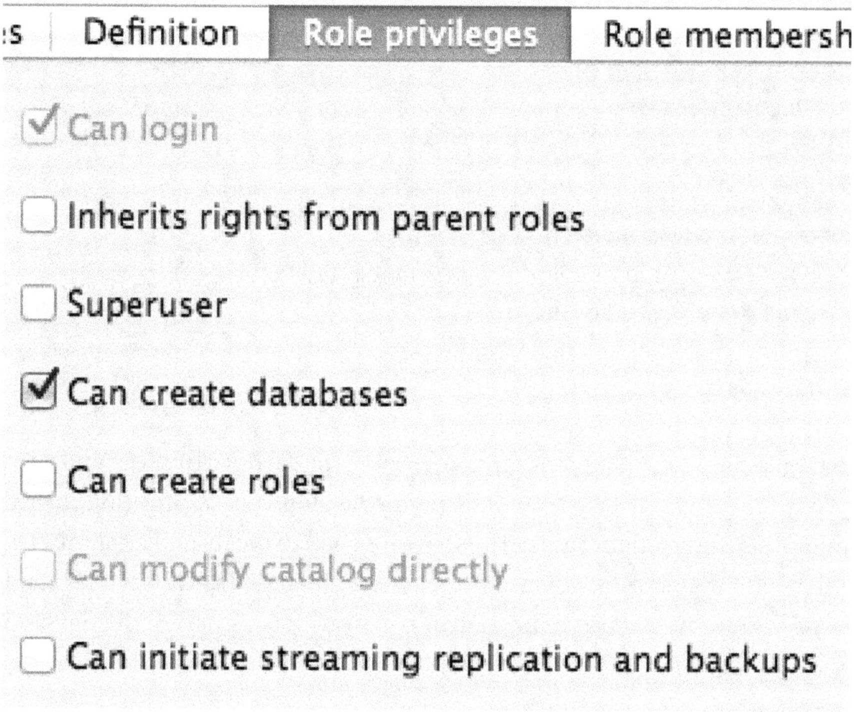

:s Definition Role privileges Role membersh

Can login

Inherits rights from parent roles

Superuser

Can create databases

Can create roles

Can modify catalog directly

Can initiate streaming replication and backups

Figure 3.3. pgAdmin role options

Then, in **config/database.yml**, you add the new credentials:

```
development:
  host: localhost
  adapter: postgresql
  encoding: unicode
  database: jumpstartrails_development
  pool: 5
  username: jumpstartrails
  password: your password

test:
  host: localhost
  adapter: postgresql
  encoding: unicode
  database: jumpstartrails_test
  pool: 5
  username: jumpstartrails
  password: your password
```

```
production:
  host: localhost
  adapter: postgresql
  encoding: unicode
  database: jumpstartrails_production
  pool: 5
  username: jumpstartrails
  password: your password
```

Once you've done that, you can run:

```
rake db:create
```

This will generate two databases for you: `projectname_development` and `projectname_test`. These two databases will help you develop your applications by running the migrations (more on those shortly) that you need to create and alter the structure of the database that supports your app. The test database (as we saw in Chapter 2), lets you add dummy data so that you can run unit tests as part of the development process.

A Little Bit of Planning

It's time to think about the main sections that we want for our app. In the previous chapter, we saw how we could put a simple app together consisting of some static pages. We'll most likely still want static pages for this app, too (Home, About, Contact). However, this time, we'll keep them as part of the app itself by storing the content in our database. The advantage in doing this is that we'll also be able to use ActiveAdmin to edit the page content.

We'll also add a blog. Once again, we'll use ActiveAdmin to enable us to manage posts on the blog. And the same goes for the portfolio section.

So with those three areas in mind, we can begin building our app.

Generating a Model

We'll start by generating a model for pages, and we can use a generator to create it for us:

```
rails g model Page title:string content:text
```

When the generator completes, you'll see this:

```
invoke  active_record
create    db/migrate/20130301081154_create_pages.rb
create    app/models/page.rb
invoke    test_unit
create    test/models/page_test.rb
create    test/fixtures/pages.yml
```

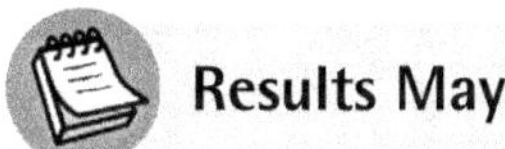

Results May Vary

The date stamp in your migrations filenames will be different, of course.

You can see that some unit test "stubs" have been created, along with the model itself, and a migration file. Great! That's our model created. Now we can migrate the database to create the tables:

```
rake db:migrate
```

Before we go racing on, however, there are a couple of points worth making. First, what happens if we don't get our database schema exactly right, first time? For example, say I wanted to add a text field called `slug` to this table. The purpose of the field would be to hold a friendly URL reference for each record in the table. That's so that we have human-friendly text in our URLs rather than a string of numbers. Let's say I also want a `blurb` field to contain a short paragraph that provides a description of the page too.

There is a way to alter table structures using migrations, even if we've already run the migration. To add another field, we just create another migration. Fire up the terminal and enter:

```
rails g migration AddSlugAndBlurbToPages slug:string blurb:string
```

This'll create a new migration in `db/migrate`. Open up the file, and it'll look like this:

```
class AddSlugAndBlurbToPages < ActiveRecord::Migration
  def change
    add_column :pages, :slug, :string
    add_column :pages, :blurb, :string
  end
end
```

So now we can run `rake db:migrate` again, and we'll see:

```
==  AddSlugAndBlurbToPages: migrating ===============
-- add_column(:pages, :slug, :string)
   -> 0.0014s
-- add_column(:pages, :blurb, :string)
   -> 0.0007s
==  AddSlugAndBlurbToPages: migrated (0.0022s) =======
```

The name of the migration (`AddSlugAndBlurbToPages`), is very important, as Rails will parse that name to create the right migration.

While we should always plan our database schema as carefully as we can, it's not always going to be possible to get *everything* right. At least now we can add more fields if we need them.

But what happens if we end up adding fields we don't need? We don't really need a `blurb` field for our static pages, do we? Our friend `rake` offers us an option to fix that. What we can do is roll back the last migration, fix it to remove the `blurb` field, and then run it again so that we only get the `slug` field we want to keep.

Let's run the rollback first:

```
rake db:rollback
```

What this does is reverse the last migration we ran. It can do this because the migration used the `change` method. The `change` method is useful because it removes the need to write both the `up` and `down` methods where Rails can figure out how to revert the changes automatically.

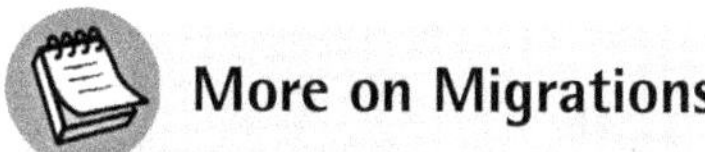

More on Migrations

You can read more about migrations in the Rails Guides[3].

What we need to do now, though, is change the migration file so that it will only add the `slug` field. We'll be able to rerun it then.

Open the migration file in your editor and change it so that it looks like this:

```
class AddSlugToPages < ActiveRecord::Migration
  def change
    add_column :pages, :slug, :string
  end
end
```

You'll also need to rename the file: **20130301082735_add_slug_to_pages.rb** (remember, the date stamp part will be different in your version). Save your changes and run the migration with `rake db:migrate` and you'll see:

```
==  AddSlugToPages: migrating ===================
-- add_column(:pages, :slug, :string)
-> 0.0009s
==  AddSlugToPages: migrated (0.0010s) ==========
```

Great! So now we have a bit more control over what fields we have in the database tables. Next, we'll want to protect our data, so we'll add some validation.

Adding Some Validation

As you've already seen, validation helps ensure that we only have valid data passed to our database. How do you decide what to validate? Obviously needs vary from application to application, and even resource to resource. However, the simple way to think about validation is this: even if you are storing blog posts, say, you still want to be sure that you've correctly added a title, some content, maybe a category, and so on. Validating now prevents potential pain later.

---

[3] http://guides.rubyonrails.org/migrations.html

The Rails Console

To help us understand this, we can introduce the `rails console`. The console provides a way for us to interact with our application from the command line. It offers both the full power of Ruby via IRB[4], and also the means to try out ideas without using the actual website.

To use it, fire up the terminal and enter:

```
rails console --sandbox
```

You'll see something like this:

```
Loading development environment in sandbox (Rails 4.0.0)
Any modifications you make will be rolled back on exit
2.0.0-p0 :001 >
```

Note the comment about changes being rolled back. That's because we started the console sandboxed in order to try things out. If we wanted to make real changes to the database, we'd just start the console without the `--sandbox` option.

First, let's see what was created for us when we generated the `Page` model. All you need to do is type `Page` into the console to examine the object. You'll see something like this:

```
2.0.0-p0 :001 > Page
 => Page(id: integer, title: string, content: text, created_at:
➥datetime, updated_at: datetime, slug: string)
```

Here, we can see the model as we created it, and also that the new `slug` field has indeed been added. Notice that ActiveRecord has created a `id` field, and a couple of timestamp fields for us too: `created_at: datetime, updated_at: datetime`. You'll always get these fields when generating models, and they're really useful, as we'll see later in the book.

Let's create a record so we can see how the process works. In console enter:

[4] http://www.ruby-lang.org/en/documentation/quickstart/

```
bad_data = Page.new(:title => 'a', :content => 'Here is some
➥content', :slug => 'my-first-page')
```

When you press `Enter` you'll see this confirmation:

```
=> #<Page id: nil, title: "a", content: "Here is some content",
➥created_at: nil, updated_at: nil, slug: "my-first-page">
```

We can confirm that this is a new record with:

```
bad_data.new_record?
```

Console will reply with: `=> true` indicating that the record has not yet been saved. You'll have probably noticed that I've used a title with a single character. That's an example of the kind of data we don't want in our database. If it's a page title, it should be long enough to actually be a title. However, there is nothing stopping us from saving the record. We'll do that now with:

```
bad_data.save
```

This will trigger a response like so:

```
2.0.0-p0 :007 > bad_data.save
   (0.2ms)  BEGIN
  SQL (73.6ms)  INSERT INTO "pages" ("content", "created_at", "slug"
➥,"title", "updated_at") VALUES ($1, $2, $3, $4, $5) RETURNING "id"
➥[["content", "Here is some content"], ["created_at", Fri, 01 Mar
➥2013 22:35:13 UTC +00:00], ["slug", "my-first-page"], ["title",
➥"a"], ["updated_at", Fri, 01 Mar 2013 22:35:13 UTC +00:00]]
   (0.8ms)  COMMIT
 => true
```

To find all the records in the table we can simply enter:

```
Page.all
```

And this will trigger the following response:

```
Page Load (0.5ms)  SELECT "pages".* FROM "pages"
 => #<ActiveRecord::Relation [#<Page id: 1, title: "a", content:
➥"Here is some content", created_at: "2013-03-01 22:35:13",
➥updated_at: "2013-03-01 22:35:13", slug: "my-first-page">]>
```

Or we could do a `find` for the specific record, like this:

```
Page.find(1)
```

This returns:

```
Page Load (0.9ms)  SELECT "pages".* FROM "pages" WHERE
➥"pages"."id" = $1 LIMIT 1  [["id", 1]]
 => #<Page id: 1, title: "a", content: "Here is some content",
➥ created_at: "2013-03-01 22:35:13", updated_at: "2013-03-01
➥22:35:13", slug: "my-first-page">
```

We'd better fix that junk title. We can run an update by finding the record:

```
page = Page.find(1)
```

And providing a proper title:

```
page.update_attributes(:title => 'Fixing the bad data')
```

If we run `Page.find(1)` again now, we'll see something like:

```
Page Load (1.0ms)  SELECT "pages".* FROM "pages" WHERE "pages"."id"
➥= $1 LIMIT 1  [["id", 1]]
 => #<Page id: 1, title: "Fixing the bad data", content: "Here is
➥some content", created_at: "2013-03-01 22:35:13", updated_at:
➥"2013-03-01 23:04:32", slug: "my-first-page">
```

What we see here, then, is that our first page contains invalid data. We don't want to allow invalid or junk data into our database, and that's why we need validations.

You can press **ctrl d** or type 'exit' to exit the console.

You've likely seen that our `Page` model inherits from `ActiveRecord::Base`. ActiveRecord is the module Rails uses to allow us to call simple methods on the model and have it interact with the database. It supplies methods to support validation as well.

ActiveRecord uses the `valid?` method to verify whether or not an object's valid. So when the validations are applied, any errors are accessed via the `errors` instance method. We get to use validation via ActiveRecord's many helpers. Not only that, but we can also use them inside our class definitions.

Let's get to some code.

In our `Page` model, we have three fields: `title`, `slug` and `content`. How might we decide to validate each of those?

- ***title***: at the very least, we should check that we've got one. We might also check its length.
- **slug** : we should definitely check that we have data, and that it only contains characters. Remember: this field will be used to create pretty URLs.
- **content** : again, we need to make sure we've got some, and perhaps check for minimum length while we're at it.

Open up your `Page` model. We'll start with `title`:

```
class Page < ActiveRecord::Base
  attr_accessible :title, :slug, :blurb, :content
  validates :title, presence: true, length: { minimum: 5 }
end
```

This says that there must be a title, and that it must contain a minimum of five characters.

Next, we'll add this validation rule:

```
validates :slug, presence: true, format: { with: /\A[a-zA-Z]+\z/,
➥message: "Only letters allowed" }
```

This ensures that our slug has a value, and that it only contains letters. Notice that we've the option to add our own (friendlier) error messages. Hang on, though—if our validation is only going to allow letters, and the slug is for our URLs, we'll need to allow hyphens, right? No problem. We can alter the validation rule like this:

```
with: /\A[a-zA-Z-]+\z/
```

Now the hyphen will be accepted.

Finally, we can copy our title validation for our content validation. It makes sense to increase the minimum length, though, as a page consisting of just two characters might look a bit odd!

```
validates :content, presence: true, length: { minimum: 100 }
```

Adding a Controller

We might as well create a controller to go with the model:

```
rails g controller pages index
```

In Chapter 2 we looked at which options the Rails generators provide for us. When you generate a controller, you'll see output similar to this:

```
create  app/controllers/pages_controller.rb
   route  get "pages/index"
  invoke  erb
  create    app/views/pages
  create    app/views/pages/index.html.erb
  invoke  test_unit
  create    test/controllers/pages_controller_test.rb
  invoke  helper
  create    app/helpers/pages_helper.rb
  invoke    test_unit
  create      test/helpers/pages_helper_test.rb
  invoke  assets
  invoke    coffee
  create      app/assets/javascripts/pages.js.coffee
  invoke    scss
  create      app/assets/stylesheets/pages.css.scss
```

In `app/controllers` we now have a new file called `pages_controller.rb`. Open it up, and it'll look like this:

```
class PagesController < ApplicationController
  def index
  end
end
```

Not very exciting, to be fair. But it doesn't need to be just yet. We've simply created an index action for now; we'll add more later.

Next up, it's time for us to create another resource.

Adding Another Resource

We have our pages. Now what about a blog? And what should it consist of? We'll start with categories and posts. Usefully, this'll also enable us to learn how to create an association between our database tables.

First, we'll create a model for categories:

```
rails g model Category title:string slug:string description:string
```

Then, we'll create one for our posts (watch out for something new here):

```
rails g model Post title:string slug:string blurb:string
➥content:text category:references
```

Creating an Association

Did you notice the addition of `category:references` above? That tells Rails that we want a one-to-many association between the `category` and `post` models. That is, *one category can have many posts*. If you take a look inside the `post` model, you'll see this:

```
class Post < ActiveRecord::Base
  attr_accessible :title, :slug, :blurb, :content, :category_id
  belongs_to :category
end
```

Rails has added: `belongs_to :category` for us. We now need to update our `category` model:

```
class Category < ActiveRecord::Base
  attr_accessible :title, :slug, :description
  has_many :posts
end
```

Here, we just need to add: `has_many :posts` to complete the association. Next chapter spoiler alert! When we generate an ActiveAdmin resource for these models, ActiveAdmin will automatically pick up the association. So when we add a new post, we'll be offered a drop-down menu to choose a category. How great is that?

You should now run the migrations with: `rake db:migrate`.

Some Rails Routing Notes

Routing in Rails is very powerful. If you read the comments in `config/routes.rb` you'll get a feel for some of the tricks you can do. You'll also notice that Rails has added a route for us already:

```
get "pages/index"
```

That's because we created a controller called `pages`. If you start the Rails server with: `rails s` and point your browser at `http://localhost:3000/pages/index`, you'll see the view that Rails created for us when we generated the controller. However, if you change the URL to `http://localhost:3000/pages` you'll get an error. That's because there isn't a specific route set for that.

We can make one, though, by adding the following to your **config/routes.rb** file:

```
get 'pages' => 'pages#index'
```

You should now be able to go to `http://localhost:3000/pages` without error.

The routes file would quickly get filled up, though, if we chose to do that for all the routes we wanted to create. But this is Rails, so there must be another way.

By default, Rails uses a concept known as **resource routing**. It allows you to easily set up all the common routes you need for a given resource. That means instead of needing to create separate routes for `index`, `show`, `new`, `edit`, `create`, `update`, and `destroy` actions, you can create a resourceful route in a single line of code:

```
resources :pages
```

We can create routes like this because browsers request a URL using a specific HTTP method. The most common methods are GET, PUT, POST, PATCH, and DELETE. Each of those methods is a request to perform an operation on a resource. So our resource route maps a number of related requests to the actions in a single controller.

REST

REST stands for **REpresentational State Transfer** and provides a way for web servers to communicate using different services.

If you look back at the training app we developed in Chapter 2, you'll see that in the **config/routes.rb** file, we have a route like this:

```
resources :posts
```

When you look inside the `posts` controller, you'll see that Rails has commented on each action to demonstrate which HTTP method that action responds to:

```
#GET /posts/1/edit
def edit
end
```

The comment also shows the type of route the action will respond to. Remember that Rails is able to deliver different formats from the action, too:

```
format.html { redirect_to @post, notice: 'Post was successfully
➥created.' }
format.json { render action: 'show', status: :created, location:
➥@post }
```

So what we have here is a Rails convention. By creating the resource, and a resource route we'll automatically get responses to HTTP requests for GET, PUT, POST, PATCH, and DELETE.

Next, we'll make sure that the root for our app points to our newly created pages controller. So add this to **config/routes.rb** :

```
root 'pages#index'
```

Then, fire up the server:

```
rails s
```

Now point your browser at: `http://localhost:3000`. You'll be greeted by a design masterpiece...

Rails Routing

You can read more about Rails routing in the Rails Guides.[5]

Adding a Test for Routes

The core idea of routing in Rails is fairly simple. It means that in a small app, such as the one we're building here, the routes we'll need are quite simple. We can (and should) still test them, though.

For example, we'll be creating a custom route for our pages, so that we can use a URL like: `http://localhost:3000/about`. It can still be tested, but we just need to change how we create the test.

A test for a regular Rails action might look like this:

```
test "should route to post" do
  assert_routing '/posts/1', { :controller => "posts", :action =>
➥ "show", :id => "1" }
end
```

We can adapt this test a little, for our `pages` controller. But where would we put this test? Well, since controllers handle traffic through our app, and controller tests are known as *functional* tests, that's where we should put our routing tests.

Take a look inside **test/controllers** and you'll see that Rails has already created a file called **pages_controller_test.rb**. Inside you'll find a test like this:

[5] http://guides.rubyonrails.org/routing.html

```
test "should get index" do
    get :index
    assert_response :success
end
```

So we can now begin to add our simple route test. Looking at the example above, we'll try:

```
test "should route to page" do
    assert_routing '/pages/1', { :controller => "pages", :action =>
➥ "show", :id => "1"}
end
```

If we were to run that test (`rake test:functionals`) it would pass with flying colors. That's because we have the route `resources :pages` already set up. However, if we want routes to our pages that allow URLs such as `http://localhost:3000/about` to work we need a slightly different test:

```
test "should route to about page" do
    assert_routing '/about', { :controller => "pages", :action =>
➥ "about"}
 end
```

Now, when you run the tests this time, they'll fail with the error:

```
No route matches "/about"
```

Which is fair enough; there isn't such a route just yet. The other thing to bear in mind, is that our `about` route doesn't fall inside the resource routes that Rails is automatically aware of. If you refer back to the training app in Chapter 2, you'll see that in the `posts` controller we have actions for `index`, `show`, `new`, `edit`, `create`, `update`, and `destroy`. You'll also remember that to get around this problem in the training app, we created a special route using a Ruby array. Here it is again:

```
%w[about contact cv].each do |page|
    get page, controller: 'pages', action: page
end
```

If you add this to your routes file, make sure you've created an `about` action in **app/controllers/pages_controller.rb**:

```
def about
end
```

You should be able to run the functional tests again, and this time get:

```
Run options: --seed 27501
# Running tests
...
Finished tests in 0.124173s, 24.1598 tests/s, 56.3730 assertions/s.
3 tests, 7 assertions, 0 failures, 0 errors, 0 skips
```

Excellent! Now our tests pass, and we know that in order to continue testing `pages` routes, we simply need to add to the array in our routes file, and create the associated action in the controller.

Installing ActiveAdmin

At this point in our app, we have a decision to make. In a real world app you'd need to decide whether to create all the back-end admin yourself (using generators, of course), or to use a gem like ActiveAdmin. The answer lies in how much control you want to have.

If you think the app will need detailed control for admin, then you're probably better off creating everything yourself. For an app like the one we're creating here, though, ActiveAdmin can be a huge time saver. And make no mistake, it's very powerful.

One of the benefits of using Ruby and Rails to build web apps, is that there is a *huge* ecosystem of gems available to solve almost any problem your app is likely to throw at you.

This is a short book, and is intended to conclude with you having built a complete Rails app. By using a gem from that vast ecosystem, we can speed up this process considerably. That's why we are going to be using ActiveAdmin to provide an administrative back-end for creating and managing content for our app, instead of using the application controllers and writing Rails code to build the app administration.

The ActiveAdmin gem is designed to provide common application patterns (such as adding/editing/deleting records), to make it easier for developers to create back-end administration quickly and easily. It also provides administrativo login through another excellent gem called Devise.

In Chapter 4, we'll be taking a closer look at what it has to offer. For now, though, we'll get it installed and ready to go.

First, we need to add some gems to the Gemfile:

```
gem 'devise', github: 'plataformatec/devise', branch: 'rails4'
gem 'activeadmin', github: 'RubySource/active_admin, branch: 'rails4'
gem "ransack", github: 'RubySource/ransack', branch: 'rails-4'
gem 'protected_attributes'
```

Also, you'll need to change the version of the jquery-ui gem used by the application.

```
gem 'jquery-ui', '~> 2.3.0'
```

Since we are using a hot-off-the-press version of Rails, many gems are not yet supported by Rails 4 with their released versions. In this case, we have to point to branches of ActiveAdmin and its supporting gems in order to stay on the bleeding edge.

When we add new gems, we need to run `bundle install`. Next, we can install ActiveAdmin:

```
rails generate active_admin:install
```

When the install process finishes, you'll see the message shown in Figure 3.4 appear.

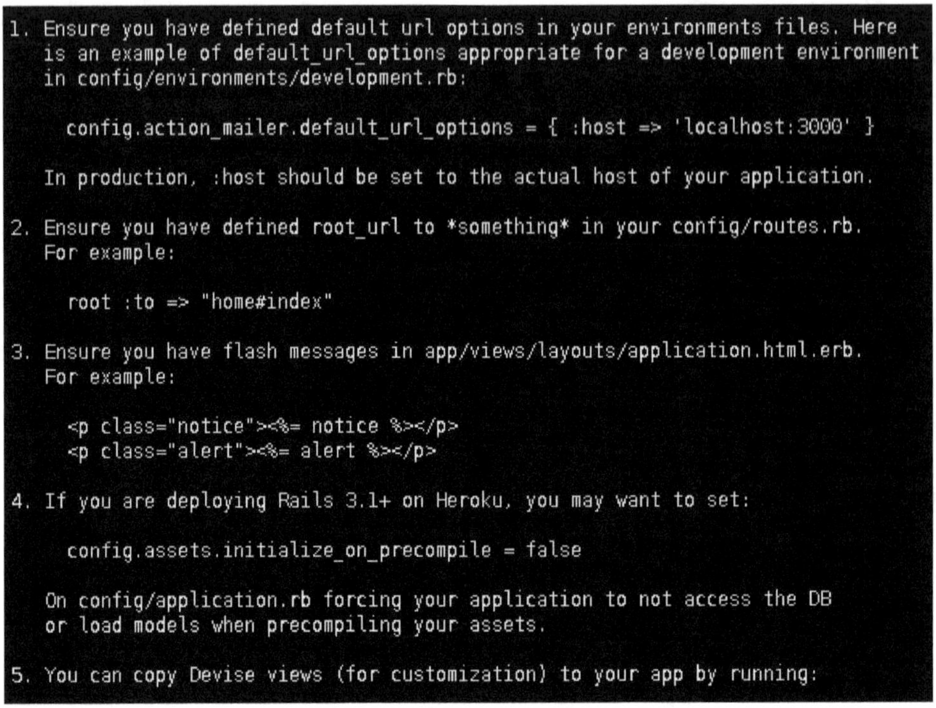

```
1. Ensure you have defined default url options in your environments files. Here
   is an example of default_url_options appropriate for a development environment
   in config/environments/development.rb:

     config.action_mailer.default_url_options = { :host => 'localhost:3000' }

   In production, :host should be set to the actual host of your application.

2. Ensure you have defined root_url to *something* in your config/routes.rb.
   For example:

     root :to => "home#index"

3. Ensure you have flash messages in app/views/layouts/application.html.erb.
   For example:

     <p class="notice"><%= notice %></p>
     <p class="alert"><%= alert %></p>

4. If you are deploying Rails 3.1+ on Heroku, you may want to set:

     config.assets.initialize_on_precompile = false

   On config/application.rb forcing your application to not access the DB
   or load models when precompiling your assets.

5. You can copy Devise views (for customization) to your app by running:
```

Figure 3.4. ActiveAdmin Install Message

Let's run through this message, line by line:

1. We don't need to worry about this just yet.

2. This is already completed.

3. This needs to be done. Open up **app/views/layouts/application.html.erb** and copy in the code shown, just above the `<%=yield %>`:

```
<body>
<p class="notice"><%= notice %></p>
<p class="alert"><%= alert %></p>
<%= yield %>
...
```

4. We'll attend to this later. For now, let's copy the line of code `config.assets.initialize_on_precompile = false` and add it to `config/application.rb`, but commented out:

```
#config.assets.initialize_on_precompile = false
```

There's a reason for leaving it commented out. We'll get to that in Chapter 6.

5. This is worth noting, but we don't need to do anything about it just now.

Remember when I mentioned the bleeding edge? Well, we have one more issue to fix before we can live with ActiveAdmin and Rails 4. In a nutshell, the `activeadmin:install` command creates the wrong migration file for admin users. To fix it, change the `db/migrate/<timestamp>_devise_create_admin_users.rb` file to:

```
        class DeviseCreateAdminUsers < ActiveRecord::Migration
          def self.up
            create_table(:admin_users) do |t|
              ## Database authenticatable
              t.string :email,              :null => false,
➥ :default => ""
              t.string :encrypted_password, :null => false,
➥ :default => ""

              ## Recoverable
              t.string   :reset_password_token
              t.datetime :reset_password_sent_at

              ## Rememberable
              t.datetime :remember_created_at

              ## Trackable
              t.integer  :sign_in_count, :default => 0
              t.datetime :current_sign_in_at
              t.datetime :last_sign_in_at
              t.string   :current_sign_in_ip
              t.string   :last_sign_in_ip

              ## Confirmable
              # t.string   :confirmation_token
              # t.datetime :confirmed_at
              # t.datetime :confirmation_sent_at
              # t.string   :unconfirmed_email #
➥Only if using reconfirmable

              ## Lockable
```

```
            # t.integer  :failed_attempts, :default => 0 #
➥Only if lock strategy is :failed_attempts
            # t.string   :unlock_token #
➥Only if unlock strategy is :email or :both
            # t.datetime :locked_at

            ## Token authenticatable
            # t.string :authentication_token


            # Uncomment below if timestamps were not included
➥ in your original model.
            # t.timestamps
          end

          add_index :admin_users, :email,
➥:unique => true
          add_index :admin_users, :reset_password_token,
➥:unique => true
          # add_index :admin_users, :confirmation_token,
➥:unique => true
          # add_index :admin_users, :unlock_token,
➥:unique => true
          # add_index :admin_users, :authentication_token,
➥:unique => true
          # Create a default user
          AdminUser.create!(:email => 'admin@example.com',
➥:password => 'password', :password_confirmation => 'password')

        end

        def self.down
          # By default, we don't want to make any assumption
➥about how to roll back a migration when your
          # model already existed. Please edit below which
➥fields you would like to remove in this migration.
          raise ActiveRecord::IrreversibleMigration
        end
      end
```

Also, delete the `db/migrate/<timestamp>_add_devise_to_admin_users.rb`file. Done? The next step is to run the database migration:

```
rake db:migrate
```

You'll see all the tables that ActiveAdmin requires being created.

At this point, restart the Rails server, and then point your browser at `http://localhost:3000/admin`. You can login in with `admin@example.com` and `password` for the password. You'll be greeted by the main dashboard, shown in Figure 3.5. It's a bit empty at the moment, but fear not; we'll be changing that as we continue to build the app.

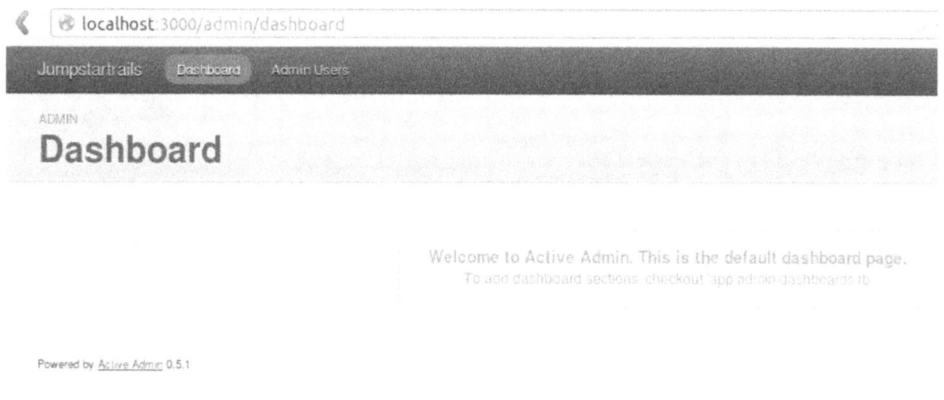

Figure 3.5. ActiveAdmin Dashboard

One thing we should do immediately is change the admin user. You can do that by clicking on `Admin Users` on the menu bar at the top of the screen, then click `New Admin User`. Fill out the details and save the new user. You can delete `admin@example.com`. This will log you out so that you can log back in with your new admin username.

Summary

We're nicely poised to add ActiveAdmin resources and make our app more useful. We've covered a lot of ground in this chapter: we've generated a couple of resources that we can use as the basis for our app; we've created some routes and added tests for them; and we've seen how we can work with our database using the Rails console, and manage the database structure with migrations.

Coming up in Chapter 4, we'll be making the ActiveAdmin dashboard more useful, and creating the resources we want for the app so we can begin to add content.

Chapter 4

Creating an ActiveAdmin Resource

We're now nicely set up to begin working with ActiveAdmin to create resources. As explained in the previous chapter we are using ActiveAdmin to create the back-end administration for our app, instead of writing the Rails code ourselves.

Before we get into ActiveAdmin, though, it's worth taking a quick look at what would be involved in creating the elements ourselves by utilizing the application controllers.

Creating Admin Functionality Manually

You can return to your training app to try out writing Rails code to develop admin resources. You'll need to add a `pages` resource as we did in Chapter 3.

So, at this stage we've got a PageController called `pages_controller`, and it contains two empty actions: `index` and `about`. For administrative purposes the convention is to use the `index` action to list all the records for a particular resource.

Following Rails conventions, we'll also need a corresponding Page model. Fire up the terminal—ensuring you're in your **training** application directory—and type:

```
rails g model Page title:string slug:string content:text
```

You'll see the output shown in Figure 4.1 as Rails creates our model with the attributes we requested.

```
invoke  active_record
create    db/migrate/20130509220301_create_pages.rb
create    app/models/page.rb
invoke    test_unit
create      test/models/page_test.rb
create      test/fixtures/pages.yml
```

Figure 4.1. Generate Page Model

You should then run the migration by typing:

```
rake db:migrate
```

We have a controller; we have a model; the last structural element is a route. Open **config/routes.rb** and add:

```
resources :pages
```

You should do this just below the `resources:posts` line in the file.

For the purposes of this exercise we'll skip over the fact that, ordinarily, we'd need to put that kind of functionality behind a login/authentication system. Instead, let's see how we'd go about getting a list of all the pages stored in the database.

Wait a minute, though: wouldn't it be useful to see how we can create a form that will allow us to add a page via our browser? It certainly would, so let's do that first.

In our **app/controllers/pages_controller.rb** we'll add a callback to share common setup and constraints between our various actions:

```
class PagesController < ApplicationController
  before_action :set_page, only: [:show, :edit, :update, :destroy]
```

In this example, we are running the `set_page` method *before* the actions in the `only` array.

You use callbacks in your controllers to write a chunk of code once, and then use it before or after any action in the controller is called. In essence this means they can be used to add actions such as authentication, logging, response compression, and also response customization. Rails supports three types of callback: before, after, and around.

The callback filters are called just before, or just after an controller action has been processed. They can run as methods inside the controller, or they're passed to the controller object when they're run. It doesn't matter which way you choose to run them—the callback will have access to information about the request, response, and other controller attributes.

Here, we're going to use a callback called `set_page` for the actions listed in the array. So now we should create the callback at the bottom of the file, and with private access only:

```
private
   # Use callbacks to share common setup or constraints
➥between actions.
   def set_page
     @page = Page.find(params[:id])
   end

   # Never trust parameters from the scary internet, only
➥allow the white list through.
   def page_params
     params.require(:page).permit(:title, :slug, :content)
   end
```

We add the `set_page` method, which will grab the id parameter out of the requested URL and search the database for the Page with that id. For example, if the URL is `http://localhost:3000/pages/123/edit`, the `id` is 123 and the `@page` instance variable will have the Page with that id. Then, the `edit` action will run and that same `@page` variable will be available.

The `page_params` method is a new Rails convention that ensures you only use the data from the request that you need. It's possible for evildoers to try to pass data and scripts to your application, and if you don't take precautions, they can hack into your server or database. The `params.require(:page).permit(:title, :slug, :content)` is one line of defense.

Creating a New Page

Now we can begin to create the actions to work with data. Add a new action like this:

```
def new
  @page = Page.new
end
```

You'll see here that we have an instance variable @page that is assigned the new object method for the Page model. We'll also need a view in **app/views/pages** named **new.html.erb**. This'll need to contain a form so we can enter the record we want to add:

```
<%= form_for(@page) do |f| %>

  <p>
    <%= f.label :title %><br />
    <%= f.text_field :title %>
  </p>
  <p>
    <%= f.label :slug %><br />
    <%= f.text_field :slug %>
  </p>
  <p>
    <%= f.label :content %><br />
    <%= f.text_area :content %>
  </p>
  <p>
    <%= f.submit %>
  </p>
<% end %>
```

We're using the form_for helper here, which creates a regular HTML form, but with a twist. The parameter used (@page) informs the method which instance variable to use when naming fields and passing field values back to the controller.

What this means is that we need another action in the pages controller. It should look like this:

```
def create
  @page = Page.new(page_params)
  @page.save
  redirect_to action: :show, id: @page.id
end
```

Here, we gather in the values entered on the form by calling our `page_params` callback action. We then use the `save` method from Active Record to save what's been passed in from the form. Finally, we redirect back to the `show` action. We'll get to creating that action next.

Showing Pages

```
def show
end
```

It looks like this method does nothing, but don't forget about the `before_action` callback to the `set_page` method that sets our `@page` instance variable!

We also need a corresponding view in **app/views/pages** called **show.html.erb**:

show.html.erb

```
<p>
  <strong>Title:</strong>
  <%= @page.title %>
</p>

<p>
  <strong>Slug:</strong>
  <%= @page.slug %>
</p>

<p>
  <strong>Content:</strong>
  <%= @page.content %>
</p>
```

So now we've created a form and the actions needed in the controller to save a new page record to the database. Next up we can create the code for listing all the pages in the `index` action:

```
def index
  @pages = Page.all
end
```

Then, in **views/index.html.erb** we can add code to display the records retrieved, as shown in Figure 4.2.

```
<h1>Listing pages</h1>
<table>
  <thead>
    <tr>
      <th>Title</th>
      <th>Slug</th>
      <th>Content</th>
      <th></th>
      <th></th>
      <th></th>
    </tr>
  </thead>
  <tbody>
  <% @pages.each do |page| %>
    <tr>
      <td><%= page.title %></td>
      <td><%= page.slug %></td>
      <td><%= page.content %></td>
    </tr>
  <% end %>
  </tbody>
</table>

<%= link_to "New Page", new_page_path %>
```

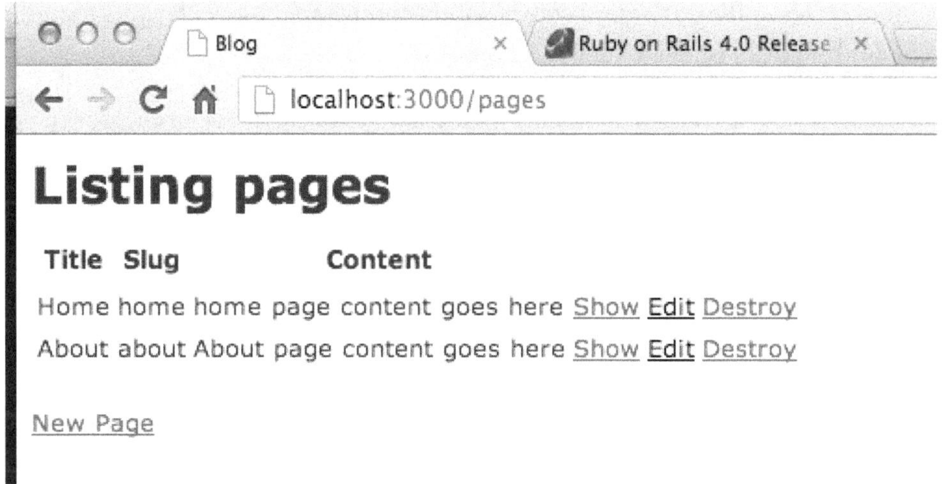

Figure 4.2. Index page listing

There's still more we could (and should) do. For example, it'd be smart to add some validation to the form, and also to turn the form into a view partial so that it can be easily included in other views. However, you've now seen the process for beginning to write the Rails code needed to create the administration area for your app.

Partials

We haven't discussed partials yet, and we won't be covering them in detail until Chapter 6. However, for now, you can think of them as a kind of include file.

Creating Resources with ActiveAdmin

Being able to generate the resources you need by writing Rails code is a skill you will need to develop. However, ActiveAdmin provides a powerful set of features that makes generating the administrative backend for our app quick and efficient. And that means we won't have to go through the process we saw at the beginning of this chapter.

ActiveAdmin has an extensive range of functionality. Here's a quick run-through of some of the key features:

- User authentication — ActiveAdmin uses the Devise gem[1] to manage user logins.

[1] https://github.com/plataformatec/devise

- Index styles — the dashboard comes with a number of possible layouts including tables (the default), grid, blocks, and even a blog view.
- Filters — you can search text fields, dates, and numeric fields for records in your database.
- Global navigation — it comes with a customizable menu bar to give you control over the admin interface.

All of those components would take time to develop, and would need to be planned carefully. ActiveAdmin already knows how to put them together, and does this by your running of the generators, not as a result of you writing lots of code.

ActiveAdmin comes with these generators so that you can quickly build the admin functions, and then edit them to suit your needs. To begin with, we'll create an ActiveAdmin resource so that we can manage the static pages of our application.

Return to your `jumpstartrails` app, fire up terminal, and make sure you're in your project folder. Then enter:

```
rails generate active_admin:resource Page
```

You'll get a reply like this:

```
create  app/admin/pages.rb
```

Then, start up the Rails server (`rails s`), log in at: `http://localhost:3000/admin` and your new pages resource will be available, as shown in Figure 4.3.

Figure 4.3. Pages resource

Clicking on the **Pages** link at the top of our Dashboard will show all the existing pages, as shown in Figure 4.4.

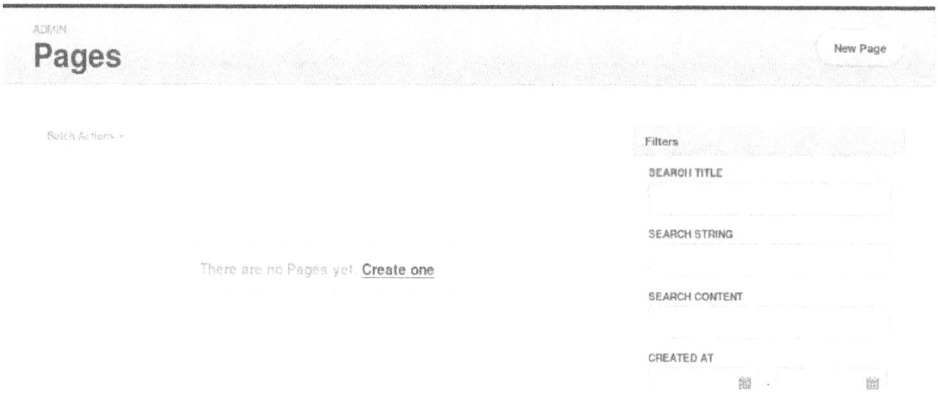

Figure 4.4. Pages Admin

Click **Create one** and you'll see a form (shown with validation messages in Figure 4.5) that enables you to create a page.

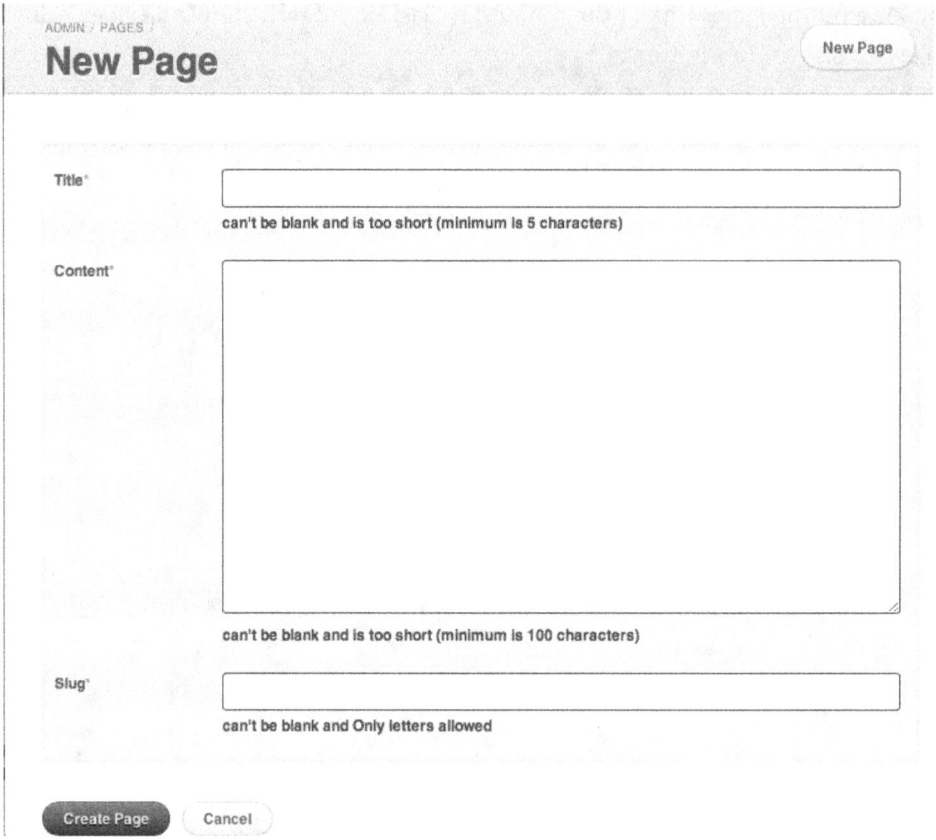

Figure 4.5. ActiveAdmin validation

Let's create an About page for our app, as shown in Figure 4.6. We'll just add some dummy content for now, but notice that the content is HTML.

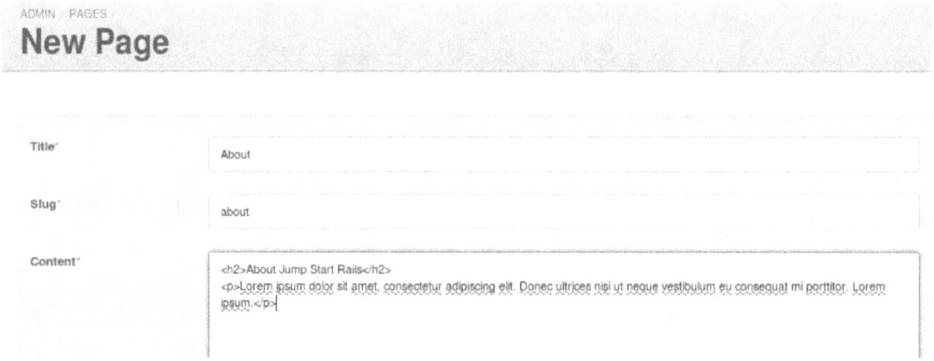

Figure 4.6. Create the About page

If you return to the list of Pages in ActiveAdmin, you'll see your newly created page, shown in Figure 4.7.

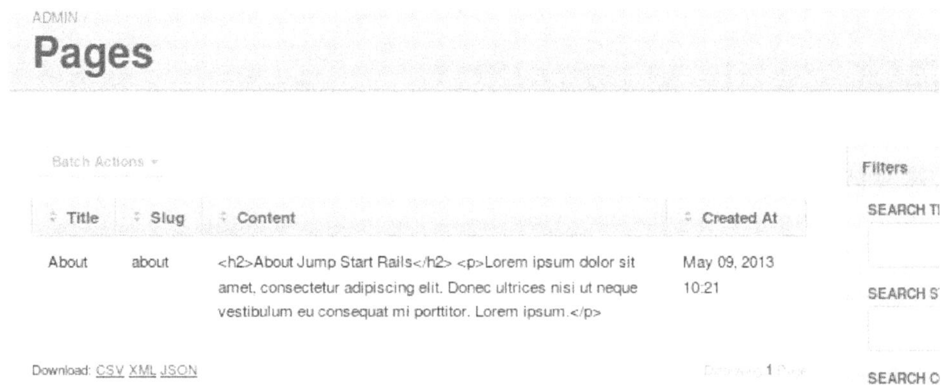

Figure 4.7. Pages listing with new page

In order to display this page in our application, we have to retrieve it from the database. Open up **app/controllers/pages_controller.rb** and change the `about` to:

```
def about
    @page =Page.where(slug: 'about').first
end
```

If you created your About page with the `slug` attribute set to `about`, this will grab that page and set the `@page` instance variable. If you're used to writing a lot more code to query your database, wave it goodbye. That's all we need in order to ask Rails to get the contents of our page for us.

Next, we'll need to add a view. In **app/views/pages** create a new file called **about.html.erb**. In it, we'll add some code to display the contents of the page:

```
<p><%= @page.content.html_safe %></p>
```

Here, we're asking Rails to display the contents of the `content` field returned from the query. I've also applied the `html_safe` method because we're storing HTML in the content field. It'll be stripped automatically by Rails unless we specifically say it's safe to display.

Do you remember that routing trick we used in Chapter 3? Well, now you'll be able to try it out. Point your browser at `http://localhost:3000/about` and your admittedly ugly page (with content in place), will be displayed.

Back to the Dashboard

Now that we've proven our admin system works, we should take a look at some of the things we can do to make the ActiveAdmin dashboard a bit more useful. The default dashboard is deliberately sparse, but there are lots of options available, so really it's a matter of deciding what you want it to contain. For now, though, we'll put something together that'll display the most recent pages we've created.

You'll notice that there's a default message being displayed. We can remove that, and add something of our own. To do that, open the **app/admin/dashboard.rb** file. All of our dashboard work is done in this file. While you're there, it's worth reading the comments in the file as you'll find some useful information. We'll put some of the commented code to use shortly. But first, we'll comment out the default message:

```
div :class => "blank_slate_container",
➥:id => "dashboard_default_message" do
  #  span :class => "blank_slate" do
  #    span I18n.t("active_admin.dashboard_welcome.welcome")
  #    small I18n.t("active_admin.dashboard_welcome.call_to_action")
  #  end
end
```

Now the default message no longer shows up on the Dashboard page.

Let's say we want to create a section in the dashboard that'll list the pages we have stored in the database. We've a choice between panels, columns, and tables. We'll try a table first, inside a section. To create a section in the dashboard, we use the `section` method. The `table_for` command is one of the most useful for our purpose. We can specify the columns we want to show, and limit how many records are displayed.

We can also restrict how many results we display in the table. Our code would look something like this:

```
section "Recent Pages" do
  table_for Page.order("created_at desc").limit(3) do
    column :title
    column :slug
    column :created_at
  end
  strong { link_to "View All Pages", admin_pages_path }
end
```

We've also added a link to go to a listing of the pages we've created with this line: `strong { link_to "View All Pages", admin_pages_path }`. The result is shown in Figure 4.8.

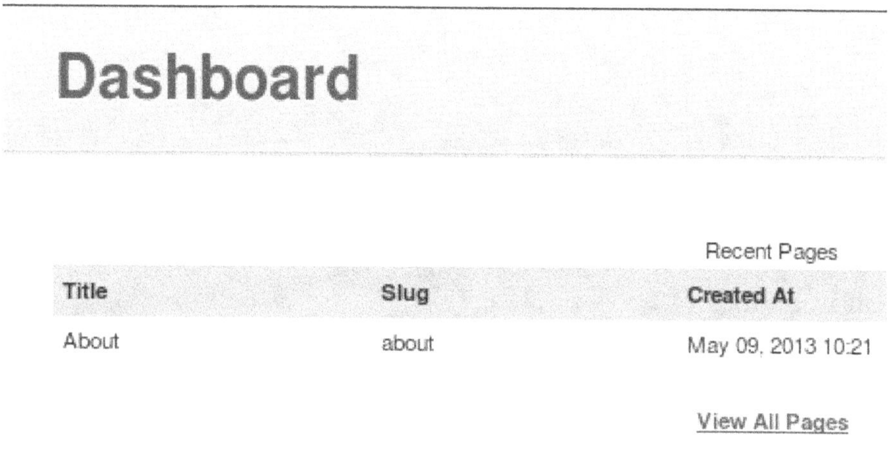

Figure 4.8. New Dashboard

Editing the Pages Listing

If you look at the listing of pages at `http://localhost:3000/admin/pages`, you'll see that the listing contains all of our fields by default. That might be what you want. However, it can also present a problem with the layout of this page. The main issue we're likely to have here is the content field. Given this will contain the entire contents of our page that we intend to display to our users, it won't be long before the listing becomes unwieldy.

The good news is that there is a way to fix it. But just to prove the point, let's make another page. Click the **New Page** button and fill in the form with whatever content you want. Mind gone momentarily blank? Throw in a few paragraphs[2] of *Lorem Ipsum*. You'll be able to delete the page or edit its contents later.

Once the page is created, return to `http://localhost:3000/admin/pages` and you'll see what I mean. As shown in Figure 4.9, we only have two pages and it already looks a bit cumbersome.

Figure 4.9. ActiveAdmin before customisation

Let's fix it. Open up **app/admin/pages.rb**. There isn't much in there, but it's where we can begin to edit the columns that appear. Add a list of the columns you want to display, like this:

```
ActiveAdmin.register Page do
  index do
    column :title
    column :slug
    column :created_at
  end
end
```

Then pop back to your browser and refresh the pages listing. You'll see that we've removed the `content` field from the listing, so it looks much tidier. However, we've now lost the options to edit and delete the pages from our listing. Thankfully, it's easy to put them back. We just need to add a call to `default_actions`:

```
ActiveAdmin.register Page do
  index do
    column :title
```

[2] http://www.lipsum.com/

```
    column :slug
    column :created_at
    default_actions
  end
end
```

Refresh your browser window, and the `view edit delete` links will be back. We've effectively removed the content field from the main listing, which makes sense because we don't need the content field in a list of all our pages.

All of these customizations to the ActiveAdmin views are possible thanks to a Domain Specific Language (DSL) supported by ActiveAdmin. This DSL is focused on making changes to the view very simple, as you've seen. This is not core to Rails, but it's a great example of what a gem can provide in terms of function and flexibility.

What is a Domain Specific Language?

A DSL is a type of programming language dedicated to a particular problem domain. Ruby and Rails are full of gems that utilize DSLs to solve specific problems. You will hear of terms like HAML, Rspec, and MiniTest, just to name a few. DSLs are great when done right. In this case, the problem domain is customizing the view in ActiveAdmin. We will continue to utilize this DSL to customize ActiveAdmin forms and views throughout this chapter.

Next, we'll generate another resource for our app. It'll be a basic blog with categories and posts. With a little bit of work, we can have our new resource in the admin area, including the automatic detection of associations we'll create between tables.

A New Resource

This is where we get some real help from ActiveAdmin. If you remember, we created `posts` and `categories` resources in the previous chapter. You'll also remember that the association was automatically picked up by Rails in the form of `one category can have many posts`. The big news here is that the association will be automatically detected by ActiveAdmin too. What that means is that the forms that ActiveAdmin generates will already be set up with a `category` field for when we add a new post.

Jump into terminal and enter:

```
rails g active_admin:resource Category
```

Follow this with:

```
rails g active_admin:resource Post
```

Then fire up the server with `rails s` if you don't already have it running and log into `http://localhost:3000/admin`. As shown in Figure 4.10, we now have our `categories` and `posts` links available for managing content.

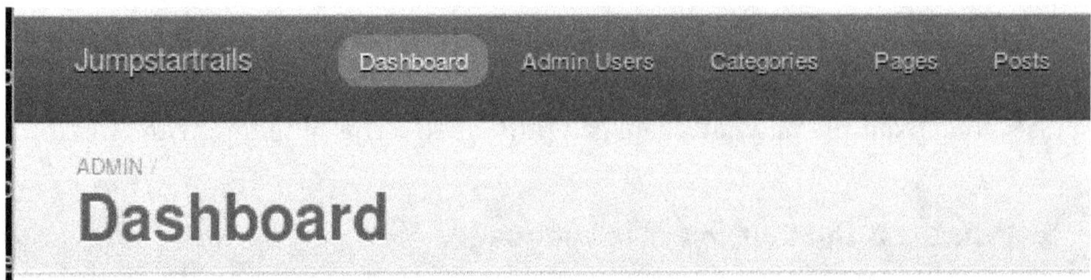

Figure 4.10. New ActiveAdmin resources

Head into the `Categories` section, and add a first category. Figure 4.11 show one I created:

Category Details

ID	1
TITLE	Getting Ready For Rails
SLUG	getting-ready-for-rails
DESCRIPTION	Covers installing Rails on a variety of platforms.
CREATED AT	February 18, 2013 22:22
UPDATED AT	February 18, 2013 22:22

Figure 4.11. ActiveAdmin category

Then, go into the posts section, and click the **New Post** button. As you can see in Figure 4.12, the association has automatically been picked up:

Figure 4.12. New post

Great! So now we can add categories and posts. That said, we don't have a way to actually display them to our users yet. Before we do so, there's still some work we can do in ActiveAdmin. For example, if you go ahead and add a couple of posts, you'll see that we have the same problem we had with the `pages` listing—namely that the main posts listing is going to get very cluttered if we don't do something to tidy it up.

To do that tidying, we need to go into **app/admin/posts.rb** and add the columns we want just as we did for pages:

```
ActiveAdmin.register Post do
  index do
    column :title
    column :slug
    column :blurb
```

```
    column :created_at
    default_actions
  end
end
```

There. That's fixed the potential issue with page bloat.

An Additional Controller

We need to create a controller for our posts resource. Let's do that next:

```
rails g controller posts index show
```

We've created the controller with two actions: `index` and `show`. It's so we have a way to show a list of posts, and then a way to view individual posts. This will also create the views we need. In Chapter 5 we'll continue to flesh out the app, but for the rest of this chapter, we'll return to the dashboard once more and add our recent posts to a panel.

Adding Recent Posts to the Dashboard

One thing we might do to make the dashboard a little more useful is to add a list of recent posts. And just to demonstrate the concept of laying out the dashboard with columns, we'll go right ahead and add an info panel too. The info panel can display more useful things than just plain text, but the purpose here is purely to demonstrate how to break up the dashboard into a columns layout.

To begin, open up **app/admin/dashboard.rb** and add a new `columns` section after the section we created before:

```
....
    strong { link_to "View All Pages", admin_pages_path }
end

columns do
end
```

It's entirely possible to nest panels inside a column, so that's what we'll do here:

```
column do
  panel "Recent Posts" do
    table_for Post.order("created_at desc").limit(5) do
      column :title
      column :created_at
    end
  end
end
```

Then we'll add a simple info panel:

```
column do
  panel "Info" do
    para "Welcome to ActiveAdmin."
  end
end
```

The whole dashboard file should now look like this:

dashboard.rb

```
ActiveAdmin.register_page "Dashboard" do

  menu :priority => 1, :label =>
➥proc{ I18n.t("active_admin.dashboard") }

  content :title => proc{ I18n.t("active_admin.dashboard") } do
    div :class => "blank_slate_container",
➥:id => "dashboard_default_message" do
    end

    section "Recent Pages" do
      table_for Page.order("created_at desc").limit(3) do
        column :title
        column :slug
        column :created_at
      end

      strong { link_to "View All Pages", admin_pages_path }
      br
    end

    # Here's an example of a dashboard with columns and panels.
```

```
    columns do
      column do
        panel "Recent Posts" do
          table_for Post.order("created_at desc").limit(5) do
            column :title
            column :created_at
          end
        end
      end

      column do
        panel "Info" do
          para "Welcome to ActiveAdmin."
        end
      end
    end
  end # content
end
```

If you point your browser at `http://localhost:3000/admin` and login, you'll now see the columns and panels. It'd be useful, though, if we could click on the title of recent posts, to view them. All we need to do is change the way the `title` column is rendered. We can employ the `link_to` helper like this:

```
column("Title"){|post| link_to(post.title, admin_post_path(post)) }
```

Figure 4.13 show what our dashboard now looks like.

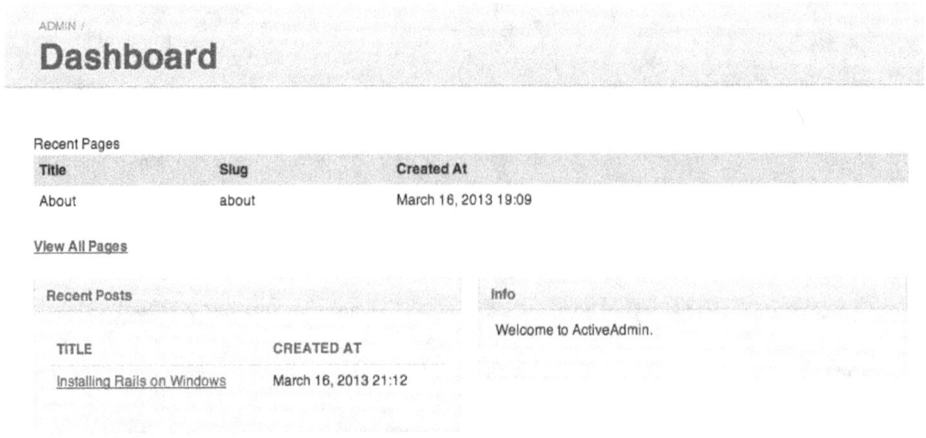

Figure 4.13. The dashboard with new columns

There are other things we could do of course, but what you want on your dashboard will depend on the app you are building. You've now seen some of the possibilities.

A Helping Hand

You'll be creating your own helper in the next chapter. However, Rails provides quite a number of helpers for working with assets, forms, dates, numbers etc. The helpers are available to all resources, meaning that you can call them in your controllers and views where you need them.

Controlling Fields on the Forms

It's possible to edit the way the form fields behave—when creating and editing a resource—in ActiveAdmin too.

If we want to add the ability to upload an image for each blog post we write, then we'll need to add an image upload field to our posts form(s). It also means we have to change the form itself, so that our browsers know that we want to be able to upload files.

Before that, we'll need to add a new field to our `posts` table so that we can store the image filename with the post. We can do that by generating a new migration to add the field:

```
rails g migration AddImageToPosts image:string
```

We'll make it a string data type because that'll be capable of holding the filename. Don't forget to run: `rake db:migrate`. In Chapter 5 we'll learn how we actually perform the image upload. For now, we just want to make sure that we've edited the `create post` form to include an image upload field.

ActiveAdmin uses a gem called Formtastic[3] to create the various forms that are used throughout the administration interface. It provides a nice clean way to create forms for your Rails apps. It's not hard to see why the creators of ActiveAdmin chose to include it as part of the ActiveAdmin gem.

[3] https://github.com/justinfrench/formtastic

To add the new form field, we need to create a fresh version of the form for adding a post. In order to do that, open up **app/admin/posts.rb**. We've code here already to manage the layout of the list of posts, and we can add our new form code to this. We'll start after the closing `end` of our columns override:

```
index do
  column :title
  column :slug
  column :blurb
  column :created_at
  default_actions
end

form :html => { :enctype => "multipart/form-data" } do |f|
```

Now we can start creating the fields. The thing to remember here is that, since we are overriding the default form, we need to ensure that we add the fields that should be available:

```
form :html => { :enctype => "multipart/form-data" } do |f|
  f.inputs 'Details' do
    f.input :title
    f.input :slug
    f.input :blurb
    f.input :category
    f.input :content, :as => :text
  end
```

Formtastic will render the fields as standard HTML text fields unless we specify otherwise. The `content` field should be a text-area, which is why we add: `:as => :text` to the field definition.

So far, the changes have re-created the form as we have already seen it, with one important difference: the form will now be file-upload aware. We can now continue with the next section of our form:

```
f.inputs 'Images' do
  f.input :image, :label => 'Post image', :as => :file
end
```

This input corresponds with our new `image` field we added in the migration. We have set the type to `file` so that we get a file browser button rendered by the browser. The whole form looks like this:

```
form :html => { :enctype => "multipart/form-data" } do |f|
  f.inputs 'Details' do
    f.input :title
    f.input :slug
    f.input :blurb
    f.input :category
    f.input :content, :as => :text
  end

  f.inputs 'Images' do
    f.input :image, :label => 'Post image', :as => :file
  end
  f.buttons
end
```

Figure 4.14 show how our form looks now.

Figure 4.14. The new add post form

Extra Functionality with Scopes

Scopes are another feature of ActiveAdmin that add a useful filtering mechanism for the records in our database. The core idea of scopes is to filter records using a particular criteria. For example, let's say we wanted to see all the posts in a certain category. We can add a scope that will provide a button link above the main listing of posts.

Let's open **app/admin/posts.rb** and add a scope to it at the beginning (this is the usual convention):

```
ActiveAdmin.register Post do
   scope :rails
    index do
    ...
```

Then, in the post model (**app/models/post.rb**) we need to add the filter:

```
class Post < ActiveRecord::Base
  attr_accessible :title, :slug, :blurb, :content
  belongs_to :category
  scope :rails, -> { where(category_id: 1) }
end
```

We've used the name `rails` because that's the first category added. If you added a different one, then just change the name accordingly. You can add more than one scope too, if you wish. Then, when you refresh your browser and click through to the `posts` resource, you'll see Figure 4.15.

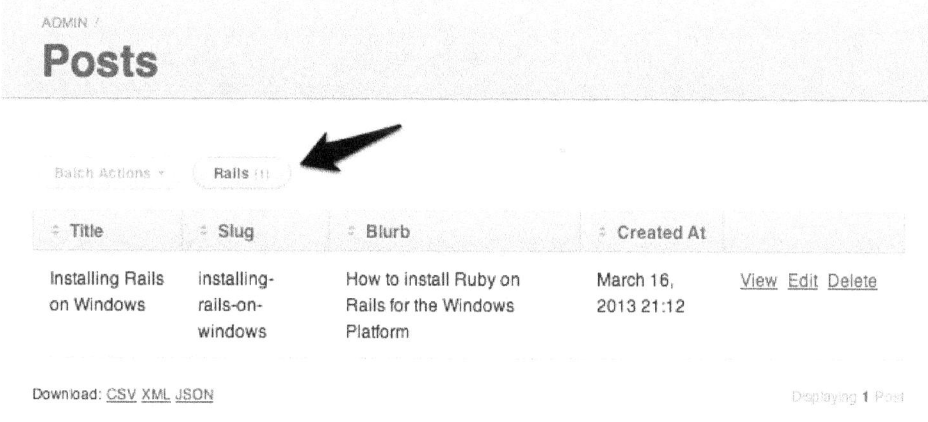

Figure 4.15. Scopes

Click the button, and you'll be taken to the `rails` category (or whichever category you've chosen). At the moment, it doesn't look particularly exciting in here, but it's not hard to imagine how useful this feature will become when you have lots of posts and categories.

Summary

We've covered a lot of ground in this chapter. We've set up ActiveAdmin so that it's easy for us to add content to our small app. We've seen how to create ActiveAdmin resources, how to change the dashboard layout, and how to change the layout of the various forms.

We've also seen how ActiveAdmin interacts with the rest of our Rails app. Elements such as the validation rules that we've added work as expected, and any new resources that are generated get automatically picked up by ActiveAdmin.

In short, we're now in a good position to continue adding features to our app, which is what we'll do in the next chapter.

Chapter 5

Adding More Features

Although it may not feel like it, we've completed major parts of our app already. Getting ActiveAdmin up and running has made it easy to begin adding content in earnest. But there are still some tweaks we can do to make working with the app a more pleasant experience. For example, you'll probably want to draw in some visitors to your site—which means we could do with some help from the Ruby ecosystem to add more features to our app.

In this chapter, we'll be adding the following:

- a gem to enable us to use pretty URLs, such as `http://localhost:3000/posts/my-first-blog-post`, rather than the Rails default style, such as `http://local:3000/pages/1`
- a gem that allows us to add metadata, such as page titles and meta descriptions, regardless of the fact that we're using layouts
- the app is desperately in need of a design makeover, and we can do that with the Bootstrap gem, so we'll implement our look and feel with a set of styles and layouts

- because we're deploying to Heroku, and it doesn't have a file system as such (more on that in Chapter 6), we'll see how we can implement file upload from inside our ActiveAdmin installation.

The FriendlyId Gem

First we'll deal with making pretty URLs. The FriendlyId gem[1] is designed to create slugs and permalinks for Active Record in your Rails app resources.

Permalinks

A permalink is a URL that points to a specific blog post or article when it's in an archive section of your site. Permalinks don't change and are therefore less likely to result in broken links to archived content.

FriendlyId has a range of useful features. We'll use it here to create those "pretty" URLs we're after. Before we tackle that, though, we need to do a bit of work to get a list of posts appearing from our `posts` index action. So open up **app/controllers/posts_controller.rb** (in your **jumpstartrails** application directory), and change the `index` action to look like this:

```
def index
  @posts = Post.all
end
```

Then, open up **app/views/posts/index.html.erb** and add the following:

```
<h1>Posts#index</h1>
<% @posts.each do |post| %>
  <%= post.title %> - <%= link_to 'Read Post', post %><br />
<% end %>
```

We're still a long way from winning any design awards but we *are* building functionality. Here, we're looping through the records that Rails returned for us, and printing them out in a simple list. We're using the `link_to` helper to create a link to the `show` action of our controller, which should look like this:

---

[1] https://github.com/norman/friendly_id

```
def show
  @post = Post.find(params[:id])
end
```

Although this is fairly self-explanatory, it's also significant bearing in mind what we want to do with the URLs. We're picking up the number value from the URL and using it to pass to Active Record to search out and return the record for us, as shown in Figure 5.1.

Title: Making Pretty Urls

Lorem ipsum dolor sit amet, consectetur adipisicing elit, sed do eiusmod tempor incidi
quis nostrud exercitation ullamco laboris nisi ut aliquip ex ea commodo consequat. Du
dolore eu fugiat nulla pariatur. Excepteur sint occaecat cupidatat non proident, sunt in

Back

Figure 5.1. Rails default URLs

Finally, we need to update the view in **app/views/posts/show.html.erb** like so (for now, at least):

```
<p>
  <strong>Title:</strong> <%= @post.title %>
</p>

<p>
  <%= @post.content %>
</p>

<%= link_to 'Back', posts_path %>
```

You may have spotted why we created a database field called `slug`. What we want for our URLs is a nice, friendly, human-readable name instead of a number, and using our `slug` field in the URL is ideal. Enter FriendlyId.

First, we must add the gem to our Gemfile:

```
gem 'friendly_id', github: 'FriendlyId/friendly_id', branch: 'rails4'
```

Notice we have to point at a specific branch of the Github repository. This is life on the bleeding edge...

Then run: `bundle install`.

Next, we need to open up **app/models/post.rb**. The FriendlyId gem requires that we extend our model to use the FriendlyId gem, and then reference the field in the database upon which we've based our slug. The `post` model should now look like this:

```
class Post < ActiveRecord::Base
  belongs_to :category
  attr_accessible :blurb, :content, :slug, :title, :category_id
  scope :rails, -> {where(category_id: 1) }
  extend FriendlyId
  friendly_id :title, use: :slugged
end
```

The line: `friendly_id :title, use: :slugged` tells FriendlyId that we want to use the slugged version of our `title` field in the URLs. The word "slugged" simply means a hyphenated version of our title that's suitable for a URL. We can safely do this because we've already created the `slug` field in the database table. Now, if you have the Rails server running, you'll need to re-start it. Then you can refresh your browser window on the `posts` page, and click one of the `Read Post` links.

Figure 5.2. Pretty URL applied

As you can see in Figure 5.2, the address bar shows that our URLs are now working. What about the admin area, though? Well, log in, and you'll see that ActiveAdmin has picked up the new URL format already, as shown in Figure 5.3.

Figure 5.3. Admin URLs

There's something else that FriendlyId looks after for us, too. Let's say that we want to change the title of a post. What would happen to the URL? Well, what we'd need is for the `slug` field to be updated to reflect the new URL. And guess what? That's exactly what happens. Why not try it out on one of your posts now? All you need to do is change the title, click **save**, and check the value in the `slug` field. You'll see that the slug is updated to a hyphenated version of the new title you've added.

That's our URLs fixed. Next, we'll look at working with metadata.

Managing Metadata

First, let's be clear about the problem we're trying to solve in this section. The metadata of a web page stores items such as title, description, character set, and the like. It's important for many things, not least of which is Search Engine Optimization (SEO). Each one of our blog posts will need different metadata values so search engines know how to categorize and rank them. Since we're storing our posts in the database, we only have one metadata section for the entire application. So how can we change the metadata (which is in the `<head>` section of our HTML page) for each post?

Well, we could write a Rails helper that dynamically swaps the contents of the metadata as each post loads. We would need to be drawing the data from our database for the meta fields, but that would be entirely possible. Or, we could turn to the Ruby gems ecosystem and see if there's anything to make the process easier.

And guess what? There is! In this instance we're going to be working with a gem called metamagic[2]. It has a single purpose, and that's to allow us to add metadata (content, keywords) for our posts and pages.

First things first: let's add the gem to our Gemfile:

```
gem 'metamagic'
```

Then run `bundle install` as usual.

The first thing we need to do is make our layout aware of metamagic. So open **app/views/layouts/application.html.erb** and change the `<head>` section like this:

```
<!DOCTYPE html>
<html>
<head>
  <%= metamagic %>
  <%= stylesheet_link_tag    "application", media: "all",
➥ "data-turbolinks-track" => true %>
  <%= javascript_include_tag "application", "data-turbolinks-track"
➥ => true %>
  <%= csrf_meta_tags %>
</head>
```

The next question is, how can we tell the dynamic sections of our app what meta we want to use? Well, if we start with pages, we just need to add metamagic values to the views. Open **app/views/pages.index.html.erb** and at the top of the file add the following:

[2] https://github.com/lassebunk/metamagic

```
<%
meta :title => "My title",
     :description => "The Jump Start Rails App",
     :keywords => %w(rails ruby on rails Rails)
%>
```

You'll no doubt recognize these as the regular metadata options. Save the view, and then fire up the Rails server if it's not already running, and point your browser at `http://localhost:3000`. Use your browser's "view source" feature to check the source code of the generated page, as shown in Figure 5.4.

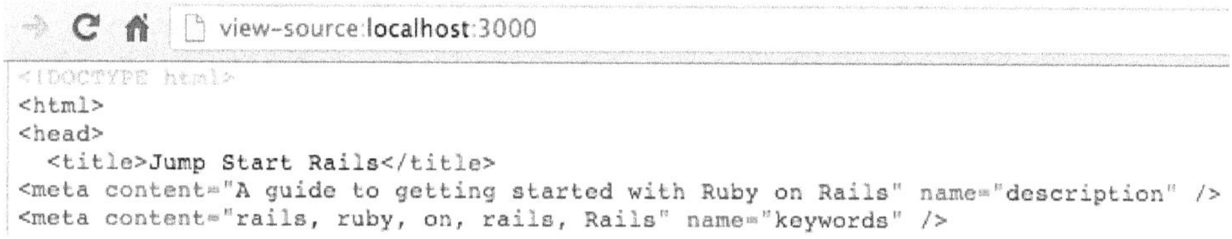

```
view-source:localhost:3000
<!DOCTYPE html>
<html>
<head>
  <title>Jump Start Rails</title>
<meta content="A guide to getting started with Ruby on Rails" name="description" />
<meta content="rails, ruby, on, rails, Rails" name="keywords" />
```

Figure 5.4. Viewing metadata

That's fine for the static pages, but what about our blog? For **app/views/posts/index.html.erb** you can do much the same as for the static pages. For individual posts we can use the data we have in our database. Open up **app/views/posts/show.html.erb** and update it to look like this:

show.html.erb

```
<%
meta title: @post.title,
     description: @post.blurb,
     keywords: %w(rails ruby on rails Rails jump start rails)
%>
<p>
  <strong>Title:</strong> <%= @post.title %>
</p>

<p>
  <%= @post.content %>
```

```
</p>

<%= link_to 'Back', posts_path %>
```

You can see here that we're using the `title` and `blurb` fields to populate the meta tags dynamically. If you load one of your posts in your browser, and then do a "view source" again, as shown in Figure 5.5, you'll see that your metadata has populated as expected:

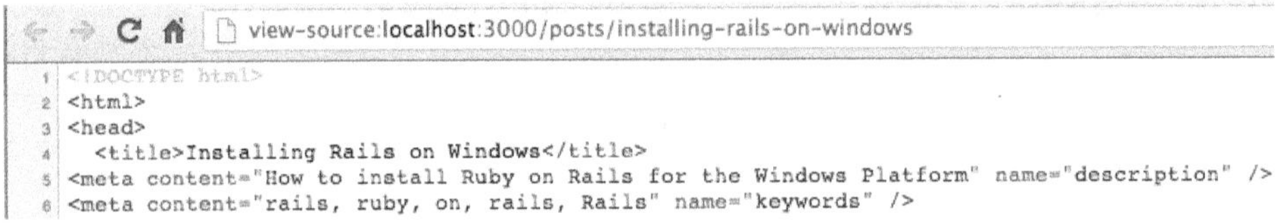

```
view-source:localhost:3000/posts/installing-rails-on-windows

<!DOCTYPE html>
<html>
<head>
  <title>Installing Rails on Windows</title>
<meta content="How to install Ruby on Rails for the Windows Platform" name="description" />
<meta content="rails, ruby, on, rails, Rails" name="keywords" />
```

Figure 5.5. Viewing metadata for posts

There's one other thing we can do, too. What happens if we don't have specific meta tags set for part of our app? Well, metamagic lets us use a set of default tags. Reopen `app/views/layout/application.html.erb` and swap the `<% metamagic %>` reference to one that includes the defaults you want to use:

```
<%= metamagic title: "My default title", description:
➥"My default description.", keywords: %w(ruby rails
➥ Ruby on Rails) %>
```

Where you don't specify the metadata you want to apply, the default metadata will be used instead. That means you can keep your SEO references consistent throughout the app.

Uploads

The next bit of functionality that will be useful to add to our app is the ability to upload images. We've done some of the groundwork for this already. If you recall, in the last chapter we added a new form to ActiveAdmin that provides an image upload input field. We also added a new field called `image` to our `posts` table in the database.

That means that we have upload-aware forms in the admin area, and a database table ready to store the filename of the upload for each post. We're going to restrict our blog to one image per post, based on the conventional blogging wisdom that there should be a supporting image for each blog post.

Initially, we'll get the upload working by uploading files to our app's public folder. Once that's happening, we'll see how to upload images to the Amazon S3 storage service.

Cloud Storage With S3

Amazon S3[3] is a simple web service that can be used to store and retrieve any amount of data from anywhere on the Web. It uses the concept of ***buckets*** to store your data. So you could have a dedicated bucket for the app we are working on. The Amazon Web Services (AWS) free tier includes 5GB of storage. You'll need to sign up for an account to use it, but if you already have an Amazon account for purchases, you can log into AWS with those credentials.

We are going to be using yet another gem from the Ruby ecosystem. This one's called CarrierWave[4]. When it comes to file uploading with Rails there are several options available. You could just use Rails, and upload the image to a binary field in your database. You'd then need to write Rails code to create an upload form, and the controller actions to run the actual upload.

Using a gem created specifically for the task makes life easier, and also provides greater options for uploading.

Paperclip

Another popular upload gem you may want to consider using is called Paperclip.[5]

Installing the Gem

Add `gem carrierwave` to your Gemfile, and then run `bundle install`. There are some optional resources you can install, but we'll get to those in a moment.

[3] http://aws.amazon.com/s3/
[4] https://github.com/jnicklas/carrierwave
[5] https://github.com/thoughtbot/paperclip

Using the Generator

CarrierWave comes with a generator so that we can generate an `uploader` class. All we need to do is provide a name for the class like this:

```
rails g uploader image
```

We're using the class name `image`, because we named the field in our database table `image`. The above command will create a new directory called **uploaders** in the **app** directory. The generated class file will be named **image_uploader.rb**, and it contains plenty of comments to help us out.

Creating an Uploads Folder

To begin with, all we need to do is make an **uploads** folder inside the **public** folder:

```
mkdir public/uploads
```

And then make sure it has write permissions so that the files can be uploaded:

```
chmod -R 777 public/uploads
```

The command will work for Unix systems. If you're on Windows *and* using Rails Installer, you'll be able to use the terminal app to do the same thing. If you aren't using Rails Installer, there's a guide here[6] to set folder permissions.

We've used the recursive switch here because CarrierWave will upload files into sub-directories organized by model and date.

Updating the Post Model

Now we can add the upload to the `posts` model. That's done by calling the `mount_uploader` method. We pass in the name—`image`—that we used above when generating the `uploader` class. Your `post` model should look like this:

[6] http://www.wikihow.com/Change-File-Permissions-on-Windows-7

post.rb

```
class Post < ActiveRecord::Base
  belongs_to :category
  attr_accessible :blurb, :content, :slug, :title, :category_id,
➥ :image
  scope :rails, where(:category_id => 1)
  extend FriendlyId
  friendly_id :title, use: :slugged
  mount_uploader :image, ImageUploader
end
```

(Be sure you add :image to the attr_accessible list!)

If you cast your mind back to the form we created in ActiveAdmin you'll remember that it is intended to store the path to an image. The model now knows about our uploaded file, and CarrierWave will also write the path to the image field in a new/edited post record, as shown in Figure 5.6.

Figure 5.6. Upload field

Uploading

We should now be able to try an upload. Either create a new post, or edit an existing one. You should be aware that different browsers render file inputs differently and unfortunately there's nothing you can do about it. The Webkit browsers (Safari, Chrome) just display a button that, when clicked, will produce a file-system browse window. When you have chosen a file, the filename will appear next to the button. In Firefox and Internet Explorer, you get an actual text field.

When you save the post, you'll see that the file path is written to the record, as shown in Figure 5.7.

Post Details

ID	3
TITLE	Introduction to Ruby
SLUG	introduction-to-ruby
BLURB	A basic introduction to Ruby
CONTENT	Lorem ipsum dolor sit amet, consectetur adipisi reprehenderit in voluptate velit esse cillum dolc
CATEGORY	Ruby
CREATED AT	March 19, 2013 22:46
UPDATED AT	March 23, 2013 19:06
IMAGE	/uploads/post/image/3/rails.png

Figure 5.7. Record with a filepath

And if you check your **uploads** folder, you should see the image has been added. There is more that we can do, though.

Scaling Images Requires ImageMagick

Being able to scale images dynamically requires the ImageMagick library. You can download a binary version for Windows[7]. If you're on a Mac, you can install via `brew install ImageMagick`, and if you use Ubuntu Linux you can install it with `sudo apt-get install imagemagick libmagickwand-dev`. Although this is an optional addition, it's very useful for creating thumbnail images dynamically — something we'll be doing later in the chapter.

[7] http://www.imagemagick.org/script/binary-releases.php

Displaying Images

How would we go about actually displaying an uploaded image? You'll need to open up **app/views/posts/show.html.erb** and amend it like this:

show.html.erb

```
<%
meta :title => @post.title,
     :description => @post.blurb,
     :keywords => %w(rails ruby on rails Rails)
%>
<p>
  <strong>Title: </strong> <%= @post.title %>
</p>

<p>
  <%= image_tag @post.image_url.to_s %>
</p>

<p>
  <%= @post.content %>
</p>


<%= link_to 'Back', posts_path %>
```

We're using a couple of helper methods here. First, we're using the ActionView helper `image_tag` that renders to a standard HTML image tag. We're also using the `to_s` method that ensures the file path we have stored is treated as a string. Finally, `image_url` ensures that Rails knows we mean to point to the **uploads** directory in our **public** folder, rather than the **assets** directory, where images would normally be stored. The results are shown in Figure 5.8.

localhost:3000/posts/introduction-to-ruby-2

Title: Introduction to Ruby

I like RubyI like RubyI like RubyI like RubyI like RubyI like R
RubyI like RubyI like RubyI like RubyI like RubyI like RubyI l
like RubyI like RubyI like RubyI like RubyI like RubyI like Ru
RubyI like RubyI like RubyI like RubyI like RubyI like RubyI l

Back

Figure 5.8. Post with image

Creating Thumbnail Images on the Fly

It'd be nice if we could display a thumbnail image of the main post image in our list of posts, wouldn't it? Well, we can. Assuming that you have ImageMagick installed, you can re-open **app/uploaders/image_uploader.rb**.

First of all we need to add another gem to the Gemfile:

```
gem "rmagick"
```

Don't forget to run `bundle install`.

In the **app/uploaders/image_uploader.rb** file, you'll see the following line commented out for now:

```
include CarrierWave::RMagick
```

Uncomment it so that our uploader knows it can call on Imagemagick for scaling operations. Next, further down the file, you'll see this line commented out, too:

```
version :thumb do

   ..
end
```

Uncomment that too, and change it to look like this:

```
version :thumb do
   process :resize_to_limit => [100, 100]
end
```

We're calling the `process` method, and also the `resize to limit` method to scale the image as it uploads. ImageMagick will do this by maintaining the aspect ratio, which is why the method is called "resize to limit"; the limits here are set to 100px.

Now, when we upload a file, we'll also get a thumbnail version, as shown in Figure 5.9.

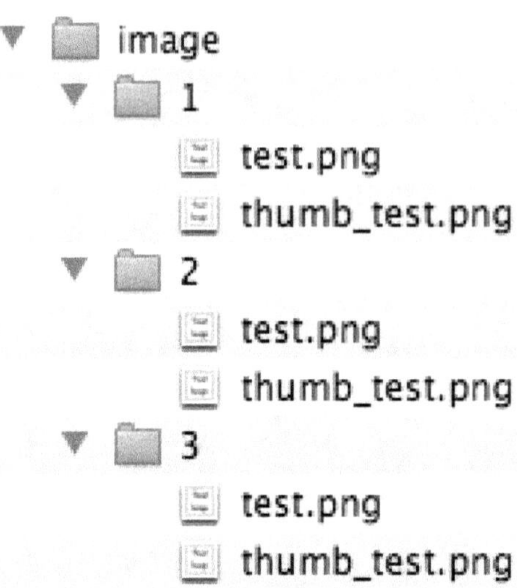

Figure 5.9. Thumbnails

Now we can update **app/views/posts/index.html.erb** like this:

```
<h1>Posts#index</h1>
<% @posts.each do |post| %>
    <%= image_tag post.image_url(:thumb).to_s %> - <%= post.title %>
➥ - <%= link_to 'Read Post', post %><br />
<% end %>
```

This is as before, except we are also calling the CarrierWave `:thumb` method to retrieve the thumbnail version of our image, as shown in Figure 5.10.

Figure 5.10. Posts with thumbs

We're in a good position now to get our uploads sent to Amazon S3 rather than to the file system. There are a couple of advantages in doing this. First, it means that deploying the app to Heroku won't be a problem, and second, even if we move where the app is deployed to, we have our uploaded resources all stored in one place.

Uploading to S3

The main tasks involved in sending our image uploads to S3 are creating an initializer, and adding some extra options to enable CarrierWave to work with a gem called Fog[8]. Fog can connect to variety of cloud resources, one of them being AWS. Carri-

[8] http://fog.io/

erWave uses that functionality to connect your uploads to a bucket of your choosing on your S3 account. Much of the complexity is hidden away, so we only have to configure a couple of things, and our uploads will work.

The first thing to do is add the Fog gem:

```
gem 'fog'
```

Then run `bundle install` as normal.

Then you should log into your S3 account and create a bucket for your app, as shown in Figure 5.11.

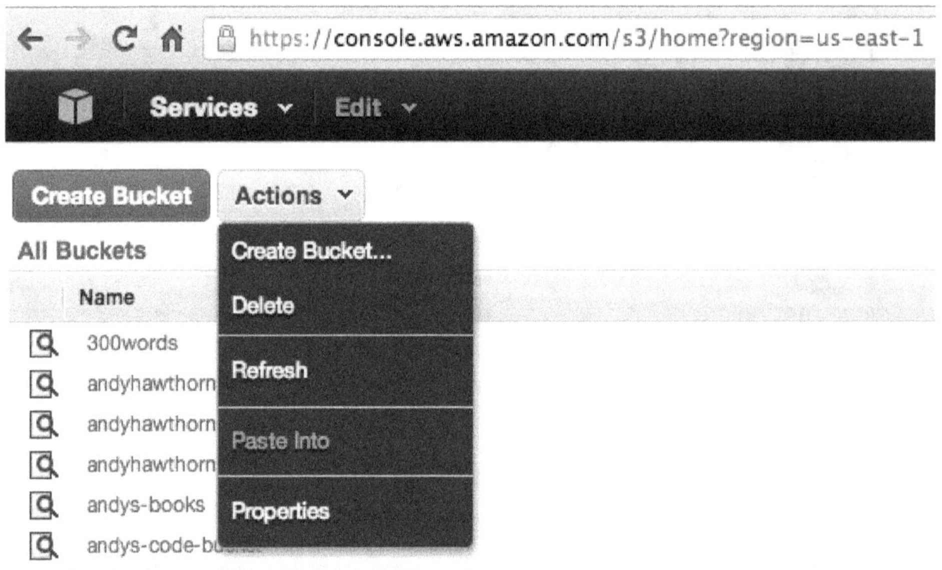

Figure 5.11. Creating a bucket

It's a good idea to do that now because you'll need the name of the bucket for the configuration options, and you'll also need your S3 credentials for the initializer code (you can find them if you click your name in the upper right-hand corner of the AWS console and choose "Security Credentials").

Next, we need to create a new file in **app/config/initializers** called **carrierwave.rb**. And you'll need to add the following to it:

```
CarrierWave.configure do |config|
     config.fog_credentials = {
    :provider                 => 'AWS',
➥# required
    :aws_access_key_id        => 'your access id',
➥# required
    :aws_secret_access_key    => 'your secret key',
➥# required
    :region                   => 'eu-west-1',
➥# optional, defaults to 'us-east-1'
    :host                     => 's3.example.com',
➥# optional, defaults to nil
    :endpoint                 => 'https://s3.example.com:8080'
➥ # optional, defaults to nil
  }
  config.fog_directory  = 'your bucket name'
➥# required
  config.fog_public     = false
➥# optional, defaults to true
  config.fog_attributes = {'Cache-Control'=>'max-age=315576000'}
➥# optional, defaults to {}

end
```

Now we can update the uploader class to use Fog. Open up **app/uploaders/image_uploader.rb** and change the top section of the file like this:

```
class ImageUploader < CarrierWave::Uploader::Base


  include CarrierWave::RMagick
  include CarrierWave::MimeTypes
  process :set_content_type
  # Include the Sprockets helpers for Rails 3.1+ asset pipeline
➥ compatibility:
  # include Sprockets::Helpers::RailsHelper
  # include Sprockets::Helpers::IsolatedHelper

  # Choose what kind of storage to use for this uploader:
  storage :fog
```

There are a couple of important differences here. First, we've added the call to CarrierWave MimeTypes along with the `set_content_type` option to make sure that the correct MIME type is set for the image. We've also told CarrierWave that we want to use Fog for storage, meaning that CarrierWave will pass the upload procedure to Fog for sending to S3.

You can restart the server now, log back into your admin area, and edit one of your posts. This time, when you click the **Update** button, the file path still gets written to the database, and the upload still runs. The crucial difference now is that the file path will be a URL to the file on your S3 account, and the file you chose will be uploaded to your nominated bucket.

Creating a Layout with Bootstrap

It's high time we did something with our look and feel, isn't it? We've already seen how to utilize Bootstrap[9] in Chapter 2. We'll employ it here too, but this time we'll see how we can use it to work with different layouts for different parts of our app. First we need to install the bootstrap-sass gem[10]. Add `gem 'bootstrap-sass'` to your Gemfile and then run `bundle install`.

Next, we'll create a layout specific to the `pages` resource in our app. In **app/views/layouts** , create a new file called **pages.html.erb**. If you recall, when we create a layout with the same name as a resource in our app, Rails will automatically use that layout when we call any actions in the pages controller.

Now we should open up **app/assets/stylesheets/pages.css.scss**. In Chapter 2 we created a new stylesheet and added all our style information in there. This time, we'll use the stylesheet specific to the resource, so that we can see how easy it is to create different layouts for our app resources.

In **pages.css.scss** add the links for Bootstrap:

```
@import "bootstrap";
@import "bootstrap-responsive";
```

This effectively installs the Bootstrap styles into the app. Bootstrap also has some behaviour that we need to include with our application JavaScript. Open **app/assets/javascripts/application.js** and add the following to the end of the file:

---

[9] http://twitter.github.com/bootstrap/

[10] https://github.com/thomas-mcdonald/bootstrap-sass

```
//= require bootstrap
```

For pages we'll use the "Justified Nav[11]"sample Bootstrap layout. There are some style rules to add to **app/assets/stylesheets/pages.css.scss** starting with the main layout sections:

```
body {
  padding-top: 20px;
  padding-bottom: 60px;
}

/* Custom container */
.container {
  margin: 0 auto;
  max-width: 1000px;
}
.container > hr {
  margin: 60px 0;
}

/* Main marketing message and sign up button */
.jumbotron {
  margin: 80px 0;
  text-align: center;
}
.jumbotron h1 {
  font-size: 100px;
  line-height: 1;
}
.jumbotron .lead {
  font-size: 24px;
  line-height: 1.25;
}
.jumbotron .btn {
  font-size: 21px;
  padding: 14px 24px;
}

/* Supporting marketing content */
.marketing {
  margin: 60px 0;
```

[11] http://twitter.github.com/bootstrap/examples/justified-nav.html

```
}
.marketing p + h4 {
  margin-top: 28px;
}
```

Next, we'll add styles for the navigation bar:

```
/* Customize navbar links to fill the entire space of the .navbar */
.navbar .navbar-inner {
  padding: 0;
}
.navbar .nav {
  margin: 0;
  display: table;
  width: 100%;
}
.navbar .nav li {
  display: table-cell;
  width: 1%;
  float: none;
}
.navbar .nav li a {
  font-weight: bold;
  text-align: center;
  border-left: 1px solid rgba(255,255,255,.75);
  border-right: 1px solid rgba(0,0,0,.1);
}
.navbar .nav li:first-child a {
  border-left: 0;
  border-radius: 3px 0 0 3px;
}
.navbar .nav li:last-child a {
  border-right: 0;
  border-radius: 0 3px 3px 0;
}
```

Now we can add our layout to **app/views/layouts/pages.html.erb** like this:

pages.html.erb

```
<!DOCTYPE html>
<html>
<head>
```

```
  <%= metamagic title: "My default title", description: "My
➥default description.",
➥keywords: %w(keyword1 keyword2 keyword3) %>
  <%= stylesheet_link_tag    "pages", :media => "all" %>
  <%= javascript_include_tag "application" %>
  <%= csrf_meta_tags %>
</head>
<body>

<div class="container">

  <div class="masthead">
    <h3 class="muted">Jump Start Rails</h3>
      <div class="navbar">
        <div class="navbar-inner">
          <div class="container">
            <ul class="nav">
              <%= nav_link 'Home', root_path %>
              <%= nav_link 'About', about_path %>
              <%= nav_link 'Blog', posts_path %>
           </ul>
          </div>
        </div>
      </div><!-- /.navbar -->
   </div>

  <%= yield %>
  <hr>

  <div class="footer">
    <p>&copy; Jump Start Rails 2013</p>
  </div>
</div> <!-- /container -->

</body>
</html>
```

Most of this is straightforward HTML, apart from a call to a custom helper, which we'll get to right now.

A Custom Helper

Let's take a look at what `<%= nav_link 'Home', root_path %>` does. We need a way to indicate to the user which page in the navigation is "active". For example, if the user is on the About page, the **About** link in the navigation should be highlighted. The best way to do this is with a CSS class, which we'll call `active`.

The problem we have is how to inform our regular HTML nav bar which page the user has clicked on. Our pages are not static HTML files, so we can't just manually change this for each page. We need a Rails helper to sort out the problem.

What we want is for each link in the nav bar to have a unique value that we can pass to our helper. The helper will then decide which page we are on, and send a string back that writes the CSS class reference where it's needed.

In each `<li>` of the menu list, we have a call to a helper called `nav_link`.

Open **app/helpers/application_helper.rb** and add the following:

```
module ApplicationHelper
  def nav_link(link_text, link_path)
    class_name = current_page?(link_path) ? 'active' : ''
    content_tag(:li, :class => class_name) do
      link_to link_text, link_path
    end
  end
end
```

Our helper is passed two parameters: the link text, and the path. Then we check to see if we are on the current page using the rails built-in helper called `current_page`. Next, we use the Rails `content_tag` helper to return the HTML `<li>` with the CSS class applied.

The next thing to do is log into your admin section and update the content for your index page. Save it, and then go to `http://localhost:3000` (having first started the Rails server).

When you test the links in your browser now, you should see that when you click on each page, the nav bar button is highlighted to show what page you are on, as shown in Figure 5.12.

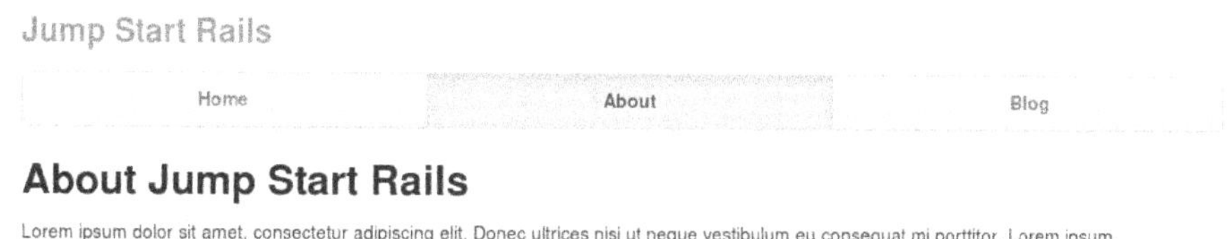

Figure 5.12. Navbar with helper working

Changing the Posts Layout

We have `pages` looking a lot nicer now, but what about `posts`? First, we can make a layout for it by adding **posts.html.erb** to **app/views/layouts**. Then, it's just a matter of choosing the layout you want. Since this is a blog, we can keep the layout more or less the same as for `pages`, but with a slightly narrower container class.

Also, we'll add a Bootstrap **hero unit** to display a link to our latest post. Here's the layout example:

```
<!DOCTYPE html>
<html>
<head>

  <%= metamagic :title => "My default title", :description => "My
➥default description.",
➥:keywords => %w(keyword1 keyword2 keyword3) %>
  <%= stylesheet_link_tag    "posts", :media => "all" %>
  <%= javascript_include_tag "application" %>
  <%= csrf_meta_tags %>
</head>
<body>

<div class="container">

  <div class="masthead">
    <h3 class="muted">Jump Start Rails</h3>
      <div class="navbar">
        <div class="navbar-inner">
          <div class="container">
            <ul class="nav">
              <%= nav_link 'Home', root_path %>
              <%= nav_link 'About', about_path %>
              <%= nav_link 'Blog', posts_path %>
```

```
          </ul>
        </div>
      </div>
    </div><!-- /.navbar -->
  </div>

  <%= yield %>
  <hr />

  <div class="footer">
    <p>&copy; Jump Start Rails 2013</p>
  </div>
</div> <!-- /container -->

</body>
</html>
```

You can see this is the same layout as before, but you could change the layout here completely if required. You'll need to copy over the styles we have in **pages.css.scss** into **posts.css.scss**, including the Bootstrap imports. We need to do this because we're not including the **application.css** manifest file in this layout, only the posts stylesheet. That allows us to have layout specific styles if we want them.

In this example, you only need to change one style rule in **posts.css.scss**, but feel free to experiment if you wish:

```
.container {
  margin: 0 auto;
  max-width: 920px;
 }
```

That won't affect your other layouts—only this one.

Now we can alter the way **app/view/posts/index.html.erb** looks. Here's the code:

index.html.erb

```
<div class="hero-unit">
  <h2>Latest post: <%= @latest.title %></h2>
  <p><%= @latest.blurb %></p>
  <p>
    <%= link_to 'Read Post', @latest, :class => "btn btn-primary
```

```
➥btn-large" %>
  </p>
</div>
<h1>Posts</h1>

<table class="table table-bordered">
  <% @posts.each do |post| %>
    <tr>
      <td style="width:100px;"><%= image_tag post.image_url(:thumb).
➥to_s %></td>
        <td>
          <strong><%= post.title %></strong><br />
          <%= post.blurb %><br />
          <%= link_to 'Read Post', post %>
      </td>
    </tr>
  <% end %>
</table>
```

You may have noticed the new instance variable `@latest`. We need to add a new call to ActiveRecord in the controller action. Open **app/controllers/posts_controller.rb** and change the `index` action to this:

```
def index
  @posts = Post.all
  @latest = Post.last
end
```

You can probably guess what `Post.last` is doing. It simply retrieves the last record added to the posts table in the database.

We have used a Bootstrap component called a hero unit, which is nice large display block. We're also using a couple of Bootstrap classes to make our table look more polished, as shown in Figure 5.13. The Rails code is the same as we had previously, only now it's sitting inside the `<table>` structure.

More on Bootstrap

You can read more about Bootstrap typography components in Bootstrap's documentation.[12]

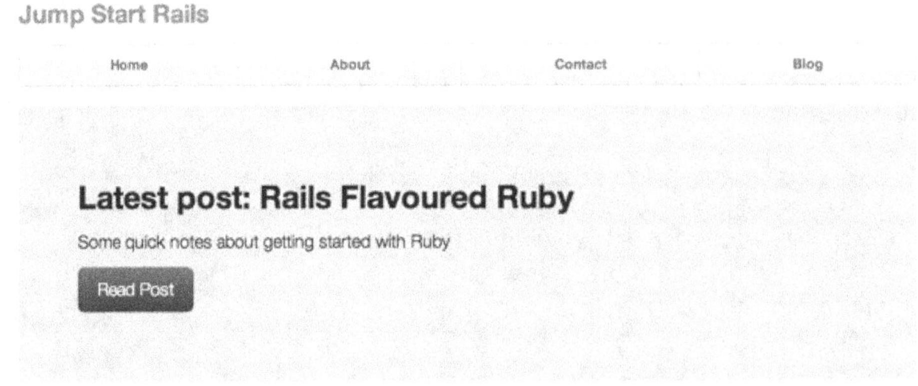

Posts

Figure 5.13. The finished posts layout

Updating the Navigation

Remember that button-highlighting trick we employed for the main navigation bar? Well, we can also use it here. While our users are reading and interacting with the blog, it'd be useful to indicate to them that's where they are. Let's change the `nav_link` application helper we made earlier in **app/helpers/application_helper.rb**. We'll add a third argument that will force the active class to be true:

```
def nav_link(link_text, link_path, force_active = false)
  class_name = (force_active || current_page?(link_path)) ?
➥'active' : ''
  content_tag(:li, class: class_name) do
```

[12] http://twitter.github.com/bootstrap/components.html#typography

```
    link_to link_text, link_path
  end
end
```

As you'll see, we can force the navigation by passing `true` as the last argument. The **app/views/layouts/posts.html.erb** layout file requires a small modification:

```
<%= nav_link 'Blog', posts_path, true %>
```

Now, whenever users are viewing your blog, the nav bar will highlight accordingly.

Controlling Images in the Layout

At the moment, our uploaded images will display with no word wrapping when we view a post. However, by applying another Bootstrap class we can make things look much nicer. Open up **app/views/posts/show.html.erb** and amend the code like this:

show.html.erb

```
<%
meta title: @post.title,
     description: @post.blurb,
     keywords: %w(rails ruby on rails Rails)
%>
<p>
  <strong>Title: </strong> <%= @post.title %>
</p>

<p>
  <p class='pull-left'><%= image_tag @post.image_url.to_s %></p>
</p>

<p>
  <%= @post.content %>
</p>


<%= link_to 'Back', posts_path %>
```

The `pull-left` class floats the image to the left, allowing the post content to wrap around it, as shown in Figure 5.14.

Figure 5.14. Image with wrapped content

We've also made sure that the `.html_safe` method is allowing for HTML content from the database to be rendered.

Summary

We now have a much more *complete* app. We've also moved closer to being ready to deploy it. In this chapter we've seen how we can upload files using Rails with the Fog and CarrierWave gems. This method provides a powerful solution for uploading images to a central repository.

We also used FriendlyId to make pretty URLs. This is an important step and means our URLs are far more user-friendly now. And the great thing is, they work in ActiveAdmin too.

The metamagic gem has solved the problem of how to add metadata for each of our resources—another important step for the marketing of our content.

Finally, we've witnessed the power of Rails layouts. By creating a layout for each of our resources, we've seen how we can have complete control over the look and feel of the app.

Coming up in the final chapter, we'll be looking at how to deploy our app to Heroku. We'll also see how to keep the content in our database synchronized between Heroku and our local version.

Chapter 6

Deploying to Heroku

In this, our final chapter, we'll add a couple more features to give us a more *complete* app, and then we'll deal with deploying to Heroku. We'll also see how to keep the Heroku database in sync with our own.

Using Partials to Add a Twitter Feed

Although probably not true of the app that we're building, it's possible that layout files can get quite busy. By now, you probably won't be surprised to learn that Rails offers a way to deal with the problem: partial templates.

Partial templates, or **partials** for short, allow you to break up the rendering process into manageable chunks. They are similar to include files in other frameworks. By using a partial, you can move the code for a particular layout component into a separate file. That's especially useful where you have a repeated layout component such as a menu bar. By moving such code blocks into a partial it helps to keep your layouts clean and tidy.

How about an example? Let's just say that we want to include a Twitter feed in our app. Twitter offers widgets[1] that make adding the required code easy. All you do

[1] https://twitter.com/settings/widgets/new

is choose a few options on the widget page and the code to embed will be generated for you. You should then make a copy of the generated code. The question is: where do we put this code?

Configuration

Search Query #rails

Options
Only show top Tweets
Safe search mode Exclude sensitive content and profanity
Auto-expand photos

Height Default (600px)

Theme Light

Link color Default (blue)

For advanced visual options, please refer to the customization documentation.

Opt-out of tailoring Twitter [?]

Create widget Cancel

Figure 6.1. Twitter widget

Go ahead and generate a widget (you'll need a Twitter account), as you'll be using the generated code in your partial. As you can see in Figure 6.1, I created a Search widget based on the "rails" hashtag. Feel free to customize your Twitter widget any way you like.

When dealing with partials, another Rails convention is to use an underscore at the beginning of the filename. So let's create a new folder in **app/views** named **partials**.

Then, inside that folder, create a new file called **_twitter.html.erb**. You should paste the code you copied for your Twitter widget into this file.

To use the partial we will put the `render` method to use. The `render` method is responsible for outputting to the user's browser.

The render Method

You can read more about the `render` method in the Rails documentation.[2]

We're now free to use our partial wherever we want it to display. Let's try it out in the `app/views/pages/about.html.erb` view. We can use the Bootstrap grid system to split the view into sections like this:

```
<div class="row">
  <div class="span9 offset3">
    <h2>Send us a message</h2>
  </div>
</div>
<div class="row-fluid">
  <div class="span8">
    form here
  </div>
  <div class="span4">Twitter here</div>
</div>
```

Then we can use the Bootstrap styles to create a form, and render our partial:

```
<div class="row">
  <div class="span9 offset2">
    <h3>About Jump Start Rails</h3>
  </div>
</div>
<div class="row-fluid">
  <div class="span8">
  Lorem ipsum dolor sit amet, consectetur adipisicing elit, sed do
  eiusmod tempor incididunt ut labore et dolore magna aliqua. Ut
  enim ad minim veniam, quis nostrud exercitation ullamco laboris
  nisi ut aliquip ex ea commodo consequat. Duis aute irure dolor in
  reprehenderit in voluptate velit esse cillum dolore eu fugiat
```

[2] http://edgeguides.rubyonrails.org/layouts_and_rendering.html#using-render

```
  nulla pariatur. Excepteur sint occaecat cupidatat non proident,
  sunt in culpa qui officia deserunt mollit anim id est laborum.
  </div>
  <div class="span4"><%= render "partials/twitter" %></div>
</div>
```

You can now see your changes by going to `http://localhost:3000/about`. You might need to add `about` to the array we have in **app/config/routes.rb** for routing purposes:

```
%w[about portfolio].each do |page|
    get page, controller: 'pages', action: page
end
```

You can see that including the messy Twitter embed code would have certainly made this view harder to read. But now that it's tucked away in a partial, it's kept the view nice and tidy. Also, we now have a partial with our Twitter feed in it that we can include anywhere in our app.

A Dash of CoffeeScript

Rails has seen various implementations of JavaScript built-in over its lifetime. It has also used different JavaScript frameworks—Prototype[3] being the favored one for a while. There was an AJAX implementation available via Remote JavaScript (RJS). There were a number of helper methods added, too, and it all got a bit tangled and messy for a while. However, Rails still scored well in its support for AJAX.

Further development in both Rails and JavaScript saw a shift to more REST-based approaches, and that made RJS and all those helpers feel unnecessary. Then, jQuery[4] took over from Prototype as the favoured way to introduce JavaScript interactions, and the Rails developers noticed. So when Rails 3.X was introduced, jQuery became the standard JavaScript framework supported by Rails.

CoffeeScript[5] was introduced to Rails in version 3.1. CoffeeScript is independent from Rails, and was created by Jeremy Ashkenas in 2009. The idea of it was to get

---

[3] http://prototypejs.org/
[4] http://jquery.com/
[5] https://github.com/jashkenas/coffee-script/

past some of JavaScript's idiosyncrasies, while retaining the good parts of the language. CoffeeScript looks like Ruby, and is written like Ruby, but compiles to JavaScript.

Let me reiterate: you write CoffeeScript instead of JavaScript. As such, if you aren't familiar with JavaScript, then you may not appreciate what you're missing (or gaining, as it were.) If you *are* familiar with JavaScript, you can still write it: just take the **.coffee** extension off of the filename and you're good to go, old school.

Getting up to Speed With CoffeScript

SitePoint has an excellent guide, *Jump Start CoffeeScript*[6], to get you started with CoffeeScript.

You'll have probably noticed that as you generated resources in your app, you were also getting files named like **app/assets/javascripts/pages.js.coffee**. Any code you put in the **pages.js.coffee** file will be available to call in the `pages` views.

Before we delve into some CoffeeScript code, it's worth bearing in mind a few syntax rules. The idea of CoffeeScript is to simplify the code you write. That means curly braces are gone. CoffeeScript uses indentation (a bit like Python if you are familiar with that), to denote code blocks. Also, JavaScript uses a lot of anonymous functions. CoffeeScript supports a shorter syntax for defining them: `->` instead of `function`. You won't be typing any semicolons either. As in Ruby, they are only necessary if you're using more than one statement on a line.

The next thing to be aware of is that you can still write jQuery code (bearing in mind the syntax rules above). If you've invested any time in learning jQuery, it'll still be useful to you as you write CoffeeScript.

Let's take a look at some code, shall we? The functionality we'll eventually add is a simple toggle link in our list of posts for the blog. When the page first loads, the blurb contents will be hidden. Clicking the link will display the blurb, and clicking it again will hide it.

First, though, we'll do something a bit simpler. Let's say we want to add a hyperlink that, when clicked, displays a welcome message to our users. To do this using jQuery

---

[6] http://www.sitepoint.com/books/coffeescript1/

we would add a class or an ID to the hyperlink, so add as the last line in **app/views/posts/index.html.erb**:

```
<a href="#" id="test_click">Just testing</a>
```

Then, in our jQuery code, we would do something like:

```
$(document).ready(function(){
  $("#test_click").click(function() {
      alert("Hello!");
  });
});
```

Or if we wanted to create a function specifically for the task:

```
$(document).ready(function(){
  $("#test_click").click(function() {
    say_hello();
  });
});

function say_hello()
{
  alert("Hello!");
}
```

What do we need to do to achieve the same thing with CoffeeScript? Since we're going to be adding our required functionality to `posts.js.coffee` we'll do our work there. Open up **app/assets/javascripts/posts.js.coffee** and add the following:

```
$(document).ready ->
  $('#test_click').click (e) ->
    do notify

  notify = -> alert('Hello!')
```

It does look a bit strange at first, but after reading it through a few times we can see where the differences are. For example, the jQuery version begins with: `$(document).ready(function(){` to make sure the DOM is fully loaded before we do any browser interactions. The CoffeeScript version looks like this: `$(document).ready ->`. You can see that most of the brackets and braces are dropped, and we can also see that the `->` is being used in place of `function`. Finally, CoffeeScript uses whitespace to delimit blocks. In other words, everything that is at the same indention level is considered to be in the same block, which may be a function, `if` statement, or loop.

Next, we can compare the `click` event code: `$("#test_click").click(function() {` and CoffeeScript `$('#test_click').click (e) ->`. By now you'll be getting the idea that CoffeeScript is more compact that regular JavaScript, and that it's more Ruby-like syntactically. In the next part of the code, we start to see real changes. First, in CoffeeScript we can call a function with just: `do notify`. The `do` keyword will immediately invoke a passed function.

Finally, the function itself is nice and clean too: `notify = -> alert('Hello!')`. Where `notify` in this case is a variable that has the actual function assigned to it. After you've allowed the code to run by accessing `http://localhost:3000/posts` in your browser, you'll see that the generated source looks like this:

```
(function() {
  $(document).ready(function() {
    var notify;
    $('#test_click').click(function(e) {
      return notify();
    });
    return notify = function() {
      return alert('Hello!');
    };
  });

}).call(this);
```

Figure 6.2 shows the result of clicking the link.

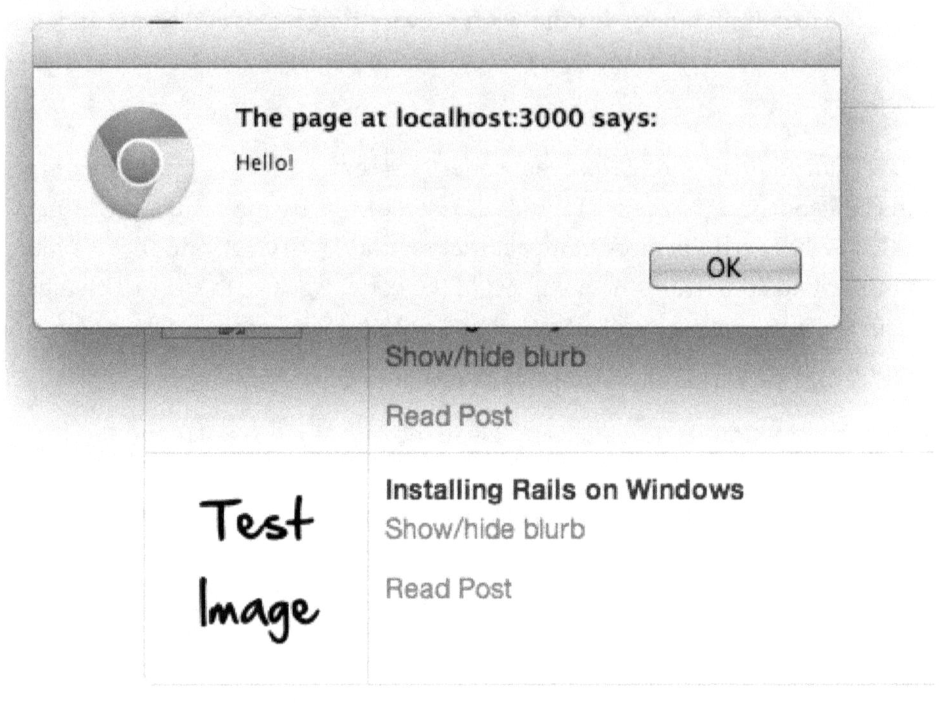

Figure 6.2. Trying CoffeeScript

Now we have a basic idea of how CoffeeScript works. Next, we'll figure out how to add the actual functionality we want.

There is a potential problem with what we're trying to do with the blurb sections: the records are coming from the database in a loop. We can't use the IDs on our HTML elements to indicate each different blurb section, because IDs on DOM elements are supposed to be unique in our markup. So, for the toggle action to work, we need a way to apply the functionality to each blurb element in the loop.

So the first thing we'll do is add some extra HTML in **app/views/posts/index.html.erb** view. The section we're interested in is where we loop through the records. Change it to look like this:

index.html.erb (excerpt)

```
<table class="table table-bordered">
  <% @posts.each do |post| %>
  <tr>
    <td style="width:100px;"><%= image_tag post.image_url(:thumb).
➥to_s %></td>
      <td>
        <div>
          <strong><%= post.title %></strong><br />
            <p class="blurb_target">
              <a href="#">Show/hide blurb</a>
            </p>
         </div>
         <p class="blurb_content"><%= post.blurb %></p>
         <%= link_to 'Read Post', post %>
      </td>
    </tr>
  <% end %>
</table>
```

We've added a `<div>` to act as a parent container for the toggle link and the `<p>` containing the actual blurb. Notice that we now also have three elements that we can access with JavaScript:

- a class called `blurb_target`
- a class called `blurb_content`
- a containing `<div>`

Next, open up **app/assets/javascripts/posts.js.coffee**. We'll start writing the code we need, starting with:

```
$(document).ready ->
```

This ensures the DOM is loaded before we begin. Then we'll hide all the `blurb_content` paragraphs, so that the user gets to decide whether to show them or not:

```
$('.blurb_content').hide()
```

Then we can respond to the click event (when the user clicks the toggle link) like this:

```
$('.blurb_target').click (e) ->
  $(this).parent().next('.blurb_content').toggle(400)
  return false
```

Although there are only a couple of lines of code here, there's quite a lot going on. First of all, we're using the jQuery `this` method, which simply lets us work with the current element. Then we use the jQuery `parent` method to search through the parent elements of our toggle link. As we pass through the elements, `blurb_content` is toggled.

What this means is that, no matter how many posts are returned in the list, we can traverse the elements, making it possible to toggle the blurb for each post. The `return false` ensures that we don't get a window reload when the links are clicked.

Watch out for Those Turbolinks

A new feature, introduced just prior to the release of Rails 4.0, is called **Turbolinks**. Its basic purpose is to try to speed up the web application.

Turbolinks saves the browser having to recompile the JavaScript and CSS you're using between each page change. It does that by keeping the current page instance alive, replacing only the body and title on each page load.

While Turbolinks does improve the speed of your app, there's an important caveat. If you're using say, jQuery and its `$(document).ready()` function, you'll find that some of your jQuery code will stop working.

Take our simple "hello" message we coded earlier. You'll be able to click the link and see the message on the blog page, but depending on where you navigate to next in the app, there's a good chance that, on returning to the blog page, the link will no longer work.

The reason is that Turbolinks is only replacing the body and title on page load, so any JavaScript that's already fired, won't fire again.

The simplest solution is to add the jQuery Turbolinks [7] gem. Add `gem 'jquery-turbolinks'` to your Gemfile and run `bundle install`.

Now, add the asset to your **app/assets/javascripts/application.js** file, like this:

```
//= require jquery
//= require jquery.turbolinks
//= require jquery_ujs
//= require turbolinks
//= require_tree .
//= require bootstrap
```

This gem ensures that your `$(document).ready()` code will work again, by re-enabling the `page:load` event. Once you've installed jQuery Turbolinks, you'll find your code works as expected.

There's another section we should add to our app: the portfolio section, which can also employ a small piece of CoffeeScript. We'll do this next.

Adding the Portfolio (or Other Content) Section

Throughout the development of the app so far, we've been referring to a portfolio section. It doesn't need to be a portfolio section, of course. It can be whatever other content you'd like to have. For example, the Jump Start Rails app uses exactly the same idea presented in Figure 6.3 for the book overview section.

[7] https://github.com/kossnocorp/jquery.turbolinks

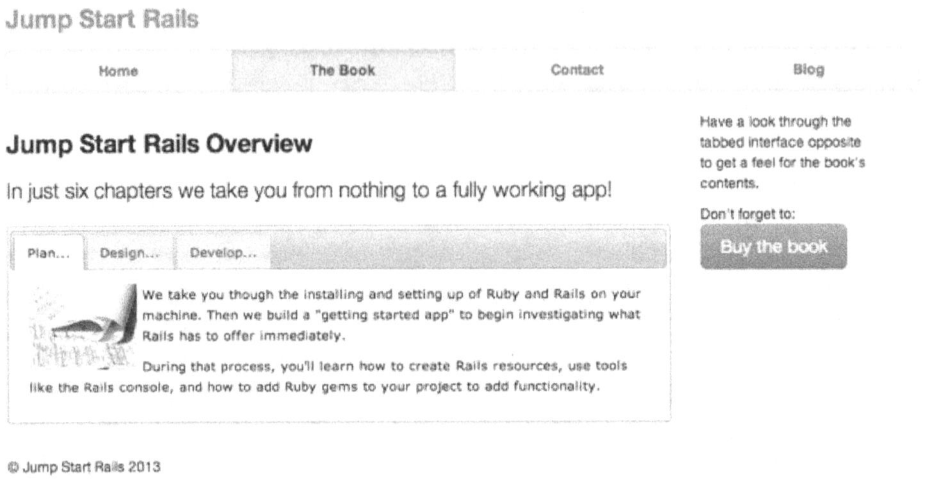

Figure 6.3. Portfolio section

You'll see that this section uses a tabbed interface, so we'll implement that here too. Remember, for the purposes of this example we'll refer to the portfolio section, but it could easily refer to any other section you want to add.

You'll need to add an extra link to the top menu in your layouts. We'll make the portfolio page a static one, rather than store it in the database. This is likely to be a page that only needs to be updated once in a while, so there's no real benefit to storing the content in the database.

You should add the new section to our `nav` too, and update the `pages` controller like this:

```
class PagesController < ApplicationController
  def index
    @page =Page.find(1)
  end

  def about
    @page =Page.find(2)
  end

  def contact
  end
```

```
  def portfolio
  end
end
```

The layouts have an extra link added:

```
<ul class="nav">
  <%= nav_link 'Home', root_path %>
  <%= nav_link 'About', about_path %>
  <%= nav_link 'Portfolio', portfolio_path %>
  <%= nav_link 'Blog', posts_path %>
</ul>
```

And don't forget to create the view: **app/views/pages/portfolio.html.erb**.

We'll use Bootstrap's grid system to get a basic two-column layout for the view:

```
<div class="row">
  <div class="span5" style="font-size: 12px;">
    content here
  </div>
  <div class="span4">
    content here
  </div>
</div>
```

We're going to add the jQuery UI tabs widget[8] for the portfolio section. We'll add the default version here, but feel free to experiment. We can add the tabs HTML markup to the left-hand `<div>` (the one with `class="span5"`) we created in the portfolio view:

```
<div id="tabs">
  <ul>
    <li><a href="#tabs-1">Nunc tincidunt</a></li>
    <li><a href="#tabs-2">Proin dolor</a></li>
    <li><a href="#tabs-3">Aenean lacinia</a></li>
  </ul>
  <div id="tabs-1">
    <p>Tab content.</p>
```

[8] http://jqueryui.com/tabs/

```
  </div>
  <div id="tabs-2">
    <p>Tab content.</p>
   </div>
   <div id="tabs-3">
    <p>Tab content</p>
   </div>
</div>
```

We can just add some dummy text for the other column for now. Next, we add the jQuery UI support files. The good news is that Rails comes with almost all the files required. It already has jQuery itself, and the jQuery UI JavaScript file. So all we need to do is add the call to the stylesheet in the `<head>` of our layout files:

```
<link rel="stylesheet" href="http://code.jquery.com/ui/1.10.2/themes
➥/smoothness/jquery-ui.css" />
```

Now we get to the CoffeeScript part. There's very little JavaScript code needed for the default functionality of the tabs; we simply need the `tabs` function. The usual jQuery code required to get it working looks like this:

```
$(function() {
    $( "#tabs" ).tabs();
 });
```

But with CoffeeScript we can get more concise than that! Open **app/assets/javascripts/pages.js.coffee** and add:

```
$ -> $( "#tabs" ).tabs()
```

The CoffeeScript version does exactly the same thing — it just needs far less code to do it. You can now try it in your browser. Go to `http://localhost:3000/portflio` and your tabbed interface should be working.

Deployment

If you have experience of working with other web development technologies such as PHP, you're probably used to FTPing to a server to upload your files. With Rails apps, you **deploy** them.

Heroku[9] is a **cloud application platform** designed to enable developers to concentrate fully on developing their apps, rather than worrying about server configurations, scaling, and so on. Heroku provides all the tools you need to begin deployment, so we'll get those installed first.

The Heroku Toolbelt

Since we're going to be deploying to Heroku you'll need a Heroku account. You can sign up for a free one[10].

We're getting closer to deploying the app now. To get ready for the process, we'll need to install the Heroku Toolbelt[11]. This is provided free of charge by Heroku, and contains key tools that you need to deploy to Heroku. It consists of:

- the Heroku client which is a command-line tool for creating and managing Heroku apps
- Foreman[12] for running your app locally
- the Git[13] version control system which you'll use to carry out the deployment to Heroku

There are separate downloads available for Windows, Mac, and Ubuntu Linux. After you've downloaded the app, the installation method is as normal for whichever operating system you use—there are no special procedures to follow.

Once you have the toolbelt installed, you'll have access to the `heroku` command from your terminal shell. To get started, fire up terminal and enter:

```
heroku login
```

You'll be prompted to enter your Heroku account credentials. Heroku will check to see if you have an existing Secure Shell (SSH) public key. If you don't, it will take you through the process of generating one, so you can communicate securely between your own machine and the Heroku cloud servers.

---

[9] http://heroku.com
[10] https://id.heroku.com/signup
[11] http://toolbelt.heroku.com
[12] http://blog.daviddollar.org/2011/05/06/introducing-foreman.html
[13] http://git-scm.com/

We are now ready to begin deployment.

Use the Heroku Docs

It's worth consulting Heroku's own documentation[14] on how to deploy an app.

Hello, Heroku

The first step to deploying an app to Heroku is to introduce Git Source Code Management (SCM) into the mix. If you've used other version control systems, you'll already know what Git will do. Perhaps you've already used Git, but if you haven't, fear not. It's easy enough to work with.

Git, like any other version control system, lets us keep *versions* of our code. When you're working on a new feature for example, you can do so on a new *branch* so as not to affect the main line of development in the *master* branch.

The clear benefit of this is that we can easily go back to a previous version of our code, or wait until we have a new feature working before merging it into our master branch.

Not only that, but Git is based on the idea of a distributed system. That means we can develop and commit locally, and then push our code to a remote server when we're ready. And that's exactly how we deploy our app to Heroku.

To begin then, we'll initialize a Git project. Fire up terminal, and make sure you're in your project directory. Then enter:

```
git init
```

Then we'll add all our project app files:

```
git add .
```

The '.' simply means add all files. Next, we'll commit our work so far:

[14] https://devcenter.heroku.com/categories/reference

```
git commit -am 'first commit'
```

Github Is Good for You

It's a good idea to create a Github[15] account. Then you'll be able to store your code there, as well as deploying to Heroku. That's one of the great things about Git, you can have more than one remote server. We'll discover how to connect to a remote repository shortly. First though, we need to create our Heroku app.

Now we've done that, we can create a Heroku project:

```
heroku create
```

You'll see your project being created with a slightly odd name like this one:

```
Creating vast-citadel-3111... done, stack is cedar
```

To give your project a sensible name, do this:

```
heroku apps:rename yourprojectname
```

Oh, and don't try to use `jumpstartrails` — that name is taken! You'll see output like this:

```
heroku apps:rename jumpstartrails
Renaming vast-citadel-3111 to jumpstartrails... done
http://jumpstartrails.herokuapp.com/
➥| git@heroku.com:jumpstartrails.git
Git remote heroku updated
```

The nice thing about that little procedure is that our Git remote repository is updated with the new name too, so we don't have to worry about it. Finally, we need to enable some features on Heroku to allow asset compilation to be successful. Type the following at the command line

```
heroku labs:enable user-env-compile
```

[15] https://github.com

You will get a message about the experimental nature of this feature, but forge on.

Deployment

We're going to jump ahead now and deploy the app. But there are a couple of issues you need to be aware of during the process. Rather than try to explain them first, we'll run the deployment and then fix the problems.

To deploy, make sure you have committed any changes, and then push to the master branch on Heroku:

```
git push heroku master
```

You'll see the deployment run through, including the gems being installed, and asset precompile running. At that point, you'll see what looks like a major error occur, shown in Figure 6.4. Did I mention we're on the bleeding edge?

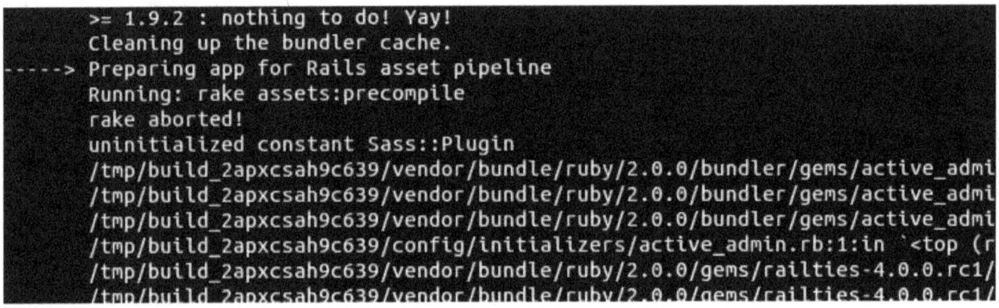

```
       >= 1.9.2 : nothing to do! Yay!
       Cleaning up the bundler cache.
-----> Preparing app for Rails asset pipeline
       Running: rake assets:precompile
       rake aborted!
       uninitialized constant Sass::Plugin
       /tmp/build_2apxcsah9c639/vendor/bundle/ruby/2.0.0/bundler/gems/active_admi
       /tmp/build_2apxcsah9c639/vendor/bundle/ruby/2.0.0/bundler/gems/active_admi
       /tmp/build_2apxcsah9c639/vendor/bundle/ruby/2.0.0/bundler/gems/active_admi
       /tmp/build_2apxcsah9c639/config/initializers/active_admin.rb:1:in `<top (r
       /tmp/build_2apxcsah9c639/vendor/bundle/ruby/2.0.0/gems/railties-4.0.0.rc1/
       /tmp/build_2apxcsah9c639/vendor/bundle/ruby/2.0.0/gems/railties-4.0.0.rc1/
```

Figure 6.4. Sass::Plugin Error

This error can be attributed to a change in the way Rails 4 handles the precompilation of assets (stylesheets, JavaScript files, images, and so on). In Rails 3.2.x, the asset pipeline was on by default, but in Rails 4 it is off in production.

In other words, Rails 4.0 presumes the assets are already compiled. Unfortunately, ActiveAdmin is not quite ready for this change. As such, we need to change a line in our **config/environments/production.rb** file. Change:

```
config.assets.compile = false
```

to

```
config.assets.compile = true
```

In order to get this change to Heroku, we need to commit and push it. At the terminal, type:

```
git add . && git commit -m "Fix asset compilation error ActiveAdmin"
```

This rather involved command is actually two commands separated by a &&. The first command adds all the changed (and untracked) files to the Git index, while the second command writes those files to the Git repository. Now, we can push to Heroku:

```
git push heroku master
```

Let me emphasize that this is not necessarily the best setting for a production Rails application, but we're making a temporary concession to keep moving. Once Heroku (as well as many of the gems we're using) solidifies its support for Rails 4, you'll likely be able to revert this change.

Web development with a community-supported framework, such Rails, often brings situations like this in front of the developer. As you grow, you'll learn how to make the call on your own.

With that change in place, type `git push heroku master` again, and you'll see something like:

```
-----> Preparing app for Rails asset pipeline
       Running: rake assets:precompile
       Asset precompilation completed (58.22s)
```

Asset Precompilation

You can read more about asset precompilation in the Rails documentation.[16]

[16] http://guides.rubyonrails.org/asset_pipeline.html#precompiling-assets

And then proceed as normal. You'll see that because we're no longer initialising on precompile the process has to complete *before* the rest of the deployment runs. That's that problem solved.

Migrate the Database

Bear in mind that there is still no data in the Heroku PostgreSQL database that has been created for your app. There is a way we can synchronize the data with our local data, and we'll get to that shortly. First, we need to create the structure of our database on Heroku. This is done by running the migrations, like so:

```
heroku run rake db:migrate
```

You'll see a message similar to Figure 6.5, followed by the migrations running.

```
Running `rake db:migrate` attached to terminal... up, run.2588
==  CreatePages: migrating ================================================
-- create_table(:pages)
   -> 0.8292s
==  CreatePages: migrated (0.8293s) =======================================

==  AddSlugToPages: migrating =============================================
-- add_column(:pages, :slug, :string)
   -> 0.0045s
==  AddSlugToPages: migrated (0.0046s) ====================================

==  CreateCategories: migrating ===========================================
-- create_table(:categories)
```

Figure 6.5. Migrating the Database on Heroku

At this point, our Heroku application should be functional!

Create an Admin User

If you remember, ActiveAdmin comes with a sample user. So we need to replace that one with a user of our own. You should now be able to point your browser at `http://yourapp.herokuapp.com/admin` and log in using: `admin@example.com` and `password`. Then create a new user and delete the sample one as we did in Chapter 4. You'll need to log back in after you have completed those steps.

Working with Data

While you're in the admin area, it would be a good time to add some pages to match the sections you've included (dummy content will do for now). If you don't, you'll get errors when you visit the front-end of the app because there's no content. If you remember, use your ActiveAdmin dashboard to create an `about` page,

It's a bit of a pain having to add the content you created locally again, but there is a way you can fix it. First, you'll need to install the pgbackup tool that Heroku offers. It can be used for free, and allows you to import and export data easily.

Installing the pgbackup Tool

To use the free month-retention tier (your backups are stored for a month), hop into terminal, and make sure you are in your project directory. Then enter:

```
heroku addons:add pgbackups:auto-month
```

You'll see a response that looks something like this:

```
Adding pgbackups:auto-month on jumpstartrails... done, v8 (free)
You can now use "pgbackups" to backup your databases or import
➥an external backup.
```

That's all there is to installing the tool. Now to actually using it.

Heroku has a number of extremely useful add-ons you can use in your app. Check the add-ons page[17] for more information.

The name `pgbackup` implies that it is a backup tool — which it is. But it has a general-purpose structure, allowing you to use it for import and export. That means it's capable of importing and exporting to/from an external database — such as your local PostgreSQL installation. And the really nice thing is that it doesn't take too much effort to run either an export or an import. The import is slightly more involved, but it's certainly not prohibitively tricky.

Exporting Data from Heroku (Production)

We'll deal with an export from our "production" application to our local development database first. Back in terminal, start the backup with:

---

[17] http://addons.heroku.com

```
heroku pgbackups:capture
```

This will produce some output like this:

```
HEROKU_POSTGRESQL_GRAY_URL (DATABASE_URL)  ----backup--->  b001

Capturing... done
Storing... done
```

Then we can use `curl` to retrieve the file:

```
curl -o latest.dump `heroku pgbackups:url`
```

This will drop the file into your project directory. You can then import the data using the `pg_restore` tool.

The pg_restore Tool

Read more about the `pg_restore` tool in the PostgreSQL documentation.[18]

The command you need is this rather lengthly one:

```
pg_restore --verbose --clean --no-acl --no-owner -h localhost -U
➥myuser -d jumpstartrails_development latest.dump
```

In this command `myuser` and `mydb` are the names you're using locally for your PostgreSQL setup.

Importing Data into Heroku

To import data from your local into the Heroku database, you first create a dump file of your local data. The easiest way to do that is use the pgAdmin tool, as shown in Figure 6.6.

[18] http://www.postgresql.org/docs/9.1/static/app-pgrestore.html

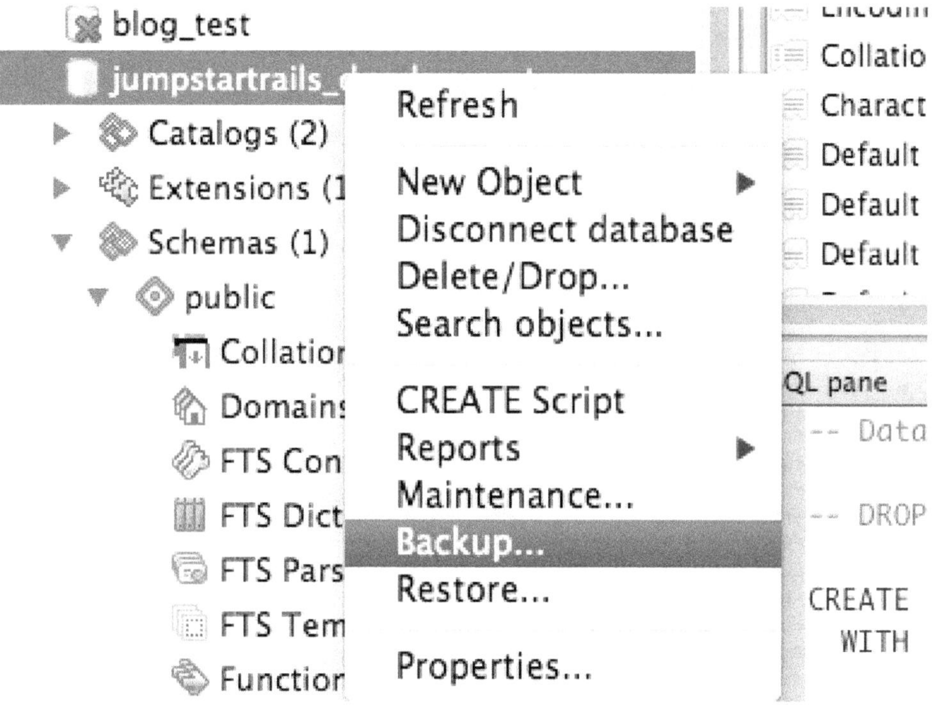

Figure 6.6. pgAdmin backup

You just need to provide a location on your machine, and a filename, and the backup will run through, as shown in Figure 6.7.

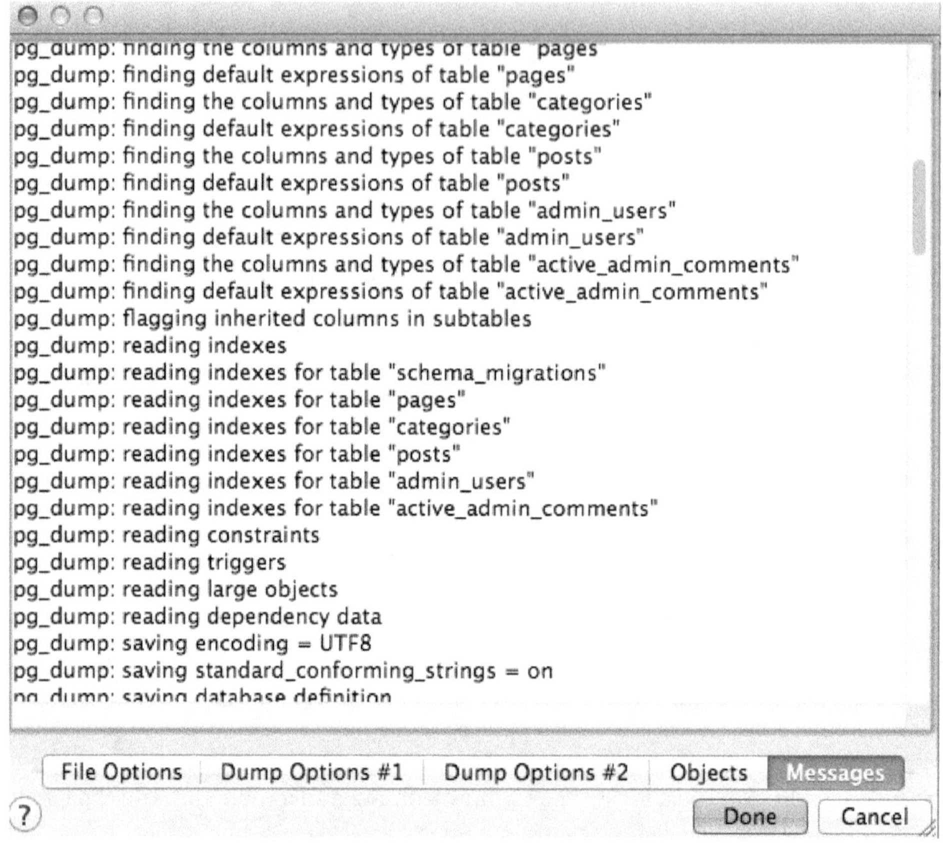

Figure 6.7. pgAdmin backup running

Then, based on Heroku's advice, the best plan is to upload the file to your Amazon S3 account. If you don't want to use your S3 account, the file must be placed somewhere with an HTTP-accessible URL. Another easy example is a public folder on Dropbox[19].

Once the file is in your S3 account, you will need to allow everyone permission to download the file, as shown in Figure 6.8. This might sound scary, but it just means the file will have the same permissions as any web accessible file.

[19] http://www.dropbox.com

Figure 6.8. Setting S3 permissions

Then, back in terminal, you can run the restore using the S3 URL of the uploaded file:

```
heroku pgbackups:restore DATABASE
➥'https://s3-eu-west-1.amazonaws.com/jumpstartrails/jsr.dump'
```

You'll then see output like this:

```
HEROKU_POSTGRESQL_GRAY_URL (DATABASE_URL)  <---restore---  jsr.dump

 !    WARNING: Destructive Action
 !    This command will affect the app: jumpstartrails
 !    To proceed, type "jumpstartrails" or re-run this command with
➥--confirm jumpstartrails

> jumpstartrails

Retrieving... done
Restoring... done
```

You'll be prompted to enter the project name, and then the backup will run. Now you have your local data pushed live.

What this means is that you can now easily transfer data between the two databases. It'll help to keep the data for your app in sync between development and production.

Adding a Custom Domain Name

Heroku allows you to add a domain name that you have registered with a provider. As long as you can access the DNS records for your domain, you'll be able to set a CNAME value that points to your app on Heroku.

Indeed, that's the first step. Log into your domain name provider and create a CNAME record that points to the www part of your domain. The value you provide for the entry is `yourappname.herokuapp.com`. The admin screens to create a CNAME record vary from host to host, but your host's tech support will help you out if you get stuck.

Then, back in terminal, make sure you're in your project directory and enter:

```
heroku domains:add www.yourdomainname.com
```

You can add more than one name if you wish. To remove a domain you enter:

```
heroku domains:remove www.yourdomain.com
```

You can read more about adding a custom domain to your application in the Heroku documentation[20].

So you can use your own domain names with your app on Heroku too. Great!

Finally...

Give yourself a pat on the back! You've built your first Rails app! Not only that, but you're now well equipped to try building more complex apps.

All that's left for you to do now is add some great content and keep improving your skills. In this chapter we've added a splash of interactivity with CoffeeScript, and we've added our Twitter feed using partials. Also, we hooked ourselves up with Heroku by installing the Toolbelt and deploying the app. We've seen how you can import and export data between your local PostgreSQL and the database Heroku provides for you.

---

[20] https://devcenter.heroku.com/articles/custom-domains

This book is too short to offer a comprehensive guide to developing with Rails. Your next step should be to take a much closer look at Ruby and Rails. They both offer a huge array of development options.

A good place to start the process of expanding your knowledge is the RailsApps Project[21]. Download the app code, and see how they're put together.

What this book has done is show you how, with just some of the basics covered, you can get an app up and running. Ruby has a huge ecosystem, and you've seen just a small area of that through the use of the gems used in the main project.

Now you've had your *jump start*, enjoy the full power of Ruby and Rails!

---

[21] http://railsapps.github.io/

www.ingramcontent.com/pod-product-compliance
Lightning Source LLC
LaVergne TN
LVHW080847170826
845678LV00006B/1738

9780987467423